RACIAL
TRANSITION
IN THE
CHURCH

RACIAL
TRANSITION
IN THE
CHURCH

James H. Davis
&
Woodie W. White

ABINGDON   Nashville

RACIAL TRANSITION IN THE CHURCH

Copyright © 1980 by Abingdon

Library of Congress Cataloging in Publication Data

Davis, James Hill, 1931–
  Racial transition in the church.
  Includes bibliographical references.
  1. Church and race relations—United States. 2. United
States—Race relations. I. White, Woodie W., 1935–
joint author. II. Title.
BT734.2.D33   261.8′348′00973   79-28817

ISBN 0-687-35280-0

MANUFACTURED BY THE PARTHENON PRESS AT
NASHVILLE, TENNESSEE, UNITED STATES OF AMERICA

Acknowledgments

We wish to thank staff colleagues in both the Commission on Religion and Race and the National Division of the Board of Global Ministries for encouragement and challenge, and to express our appreciation to both agencies for support during the time of study, though this book does not necessarily represent the policies of either agency.

Our insights have been honed by opportunities to make presentations to and to exchange views with a number of groups, especially the National Workshop on Churches in Transitional Communities, sponsored by The United Methodist Church (August 1976), the United Church of Christ Churches in Transitional Communities Consultation (October 1977), the Hartford Seminary Symposium on Church Growth and Decline (February 1978), the McCormick Seminary Workshop on Churches in Transitional Communities (April 1978), and the Joint Strategy and Action Committee (JSAC) Conference on Churches in Racially/Ethnically Transitional Communities (1979). We have also gained a great deal from regular participation on the JSAC Subcommittee on Churches in Transitional Communities and from opportunities to meet with the Virginia Conference Task Force in Transitional Communities over an extended period.

We are grateful to Winston Taylor and Doris Quinn for their careful editing, and also to the following persons who have read and commented on all or parts of the various drafts of the manuscript: Carl S. Dudley and the students in his class, Churches in Transitional Communities; B. Carlisle Driggers, Philip C. Edwards, Dalila Cruz Krueger, Barbara Lavery, Negail R. Riley, Paul Strockbine, and Samuel Wong. Doris Quinn, Diona Thomas, and Stanley Lippman typed the numerous drafts, and Linda McCargar and Martha Chavis supervised the production of the manuscript.

Most of all, we owe a debt of thanks to the pastors and lay people of the churches in transitional communities with whom we have worked over the years, especially those who generously gave of their time for interviews. Their joys and sorrows have become our own and are the raw material from which this book is fashioned.

Contents

Some Theological
and
Sociological Reflections

It is somewhat perilous to predict or to attempt to forecast the future or the needs of the future. The pace of social change in American society apparently slowed down in the 1970s, but the rate could escalate again at any time. The hapless prognosticator inevitably becomes involved in abstracting significant currents from a morass of partial tendencies, trends, and countertrends, and in assigning conceptual labels to forces which may prove to be mere will-o'-the-wisps.

Furthermore, some predictions have a way of creating their own destruction. The self-denying prophecy is the opposite of the self-fulfilling prophecy. Some predictions are unacceptable to key decision-makers; consequently, as soon as they are aware of a prediction, they set to work to avoid its fulfillment.

As we attempt to express our opinions about the future of the church in racially changing communities, we are very conscious of the many variables, the unpredictable nature of the future, and the exceptions to the rule. Moreover, as clergymen, we are cognizant that the working of the Holy Spirit is a reality that cannot be ignored—or predicted. These modest projections and proposals about the church in transitional communities are not exhaustive, but rather, illustrative.

More than six years ago we embarked on a restudy of churches in racially changing communities. An earlier study was out of print and also out of date.[1] But denominational offices were still receiving requests for assistance. New information, reflecting today's realities and tomorrow's possibilities, was needed.

In order to provide a nationwide perspective, we selected twenty cities, representative of those with the largest black populations, and prepared analyses of each. To gain an ecumenical perspective, we interviewed national denominational leaders and, where possible, talked with people in local churches of a number of denominations. Though white/black transition remained our major focus, we also studied and interviewed Asians, Hispanics, and Native Americans, to gain a broader perspective. Then, in the course of the study, "reverse transition"—displacement—emerged as a new phenomenon. This meant that another group of churches needed to be considered.

Our study is a combination of systematic and random observations during a six-year period, although it actually embraces the experiences of almost two decades of involvement in transitional communities in various parts of the country. Woodie has served and worked in racially transitional communities as associate pastor, as pastor, and as urban staff member. In recent years, as the executive secretary of the Commission on Religion and Race in The United Methodist Church, he has led consultations and hearings throughout the United States, and has conducted workshops on racism and on the ethnic church. As the research director of the National Division of the Board of Global Ministries, Jim has studied more than three thousand congregations, many of them in transitional communities. We first worked together more than ten years ago in a local planning study, and in the intervening years, we have continued to collaborate from time to time in various studies and projects.

In some ways, our interviews were exciting adventures. We met ministers and lay persons who are ministering with great skill and effectiveness. Their experiences and valuable insights have contributed to our understanding, and it is a joy to celebrate their faithfulness. In other ways, the interviews were sobering experiences. Again and again we saw the church trying to reinvent the wheel, repeating mistakes that had been made elsewhere, vacillating, dodging, denying, and trying to avoid a seemingly inevitable future.

In racially transitional communities the blatant racism of America is clearly evidenced and easily documented. In the process of transition, an area becomes defined as an area to be inhabited by black (or other ethnic minority) people—a kind of *apartheid* through social convention. Communities in racial transition epitomize the institutional racism of the nation. They are parts of a system—a self-perpetuating pattern in which prejudice produces discrimination, discrimination results in separation, and separation breeds ignorance, suspicion, hatred, and more prejudice.

Racism is the belief in the superiority of one race over other races. But the phenomenon of racism does not end with belief, for belief must be enforced or acted out in order to make its ultimate impact. Therefore, racism is systemic (institutional) as well as attitudinal (individual). Institutional racism is the manner in which racism is perpetuated and reinforced by institutions: banks, businesses, industries, schools, governments (including law enforcement agencies), and even by families and churches.

To identify the nature of racism as systemic is not to suggest that it operates apart from individuals.

> It is fashionable nowadays to think of racism as a vast, impersonal system for which no one is responsible. But this is still another evasion. Racism did not fall from the sky; it was not secreted by insects. No! Racism in America was made by men, neighborhood by neighborhood, law by law, restrictive covenant by restrictive covenant, deed by deed.[2]

As local churches of the predominantly white denominations have found themselves in racially transitional communities, they have made a sobering discovery. What they learned was that they had no answers. Their solutions have caused pain, trauma, embarrassment, and even loss of millions of dollars worth of property. These churches have had their faith challenged by problems that seemingly have overwhelmed them.

The church in the transitional community, however, need not be overwhelmed. The Old Testament speaks of the "God of Abraham, Isaac, and Jacob," who was faithful to his covenant people Israel, through the various vicissitudes of their history as a people and as a nation.

The church need not fear change, but it should seek to discover God's will in the midst of that change. "Discerning the signs of the times is the responsibility of every Christian . . . to hear, distinguish, and interpret the many voices of our age, and to judge them in the light of the divine Word."[3]

As the church in the transitional community is faced with persons of different races, languages, and cultures, it can affirm the gospel's claim that it is Good News for all people. How that Word is to be proclaimed to a particular group in a particular place may vary in style, but not in substance. The universality of the gospel is the Good News that Jesus Christ the Lord came that "*all* might have life and have it more abundantly."

All too often local congregations in transitional communities have not been prepared either to understand that change is of God, or to have sufficient resources of faith to undergird them in those times. Those congregations that have successfully met the challenge of transition in the community have, of necessity, found new riches and resources in their faith.

Faith, for the church, is anchor, compass, and calendar. As anchor, it holds the faithful people firm when winds and storms of history threaten to blow them indiscriminately here and there, dashing them furiously against the rocks of destruction.

As compass, faith guides the people of God through uncharted waters—however dangerous and unfamiliar—directing them through an unexplored wilderness of new experiences.

As calendar, faith assures them, however uncertain the times might appear, that time is in God's hands.

Finally, the church in the transitional community must hold on to its belief in hope, resurrection, salvation. The church has always understood that its beginning was in an Easter event! *Resurrection* is what the Christian celebrates! Out of darkness, comes light; out of despair, comes hope. "Hope alone is to be called 'realistic', because it does not take things as they happen to stand or to lie, but as progressing, moving things with possibilities of change."[4]

Dilemmas of Racial Transition

Thomas Jefferson, author of the immortal phrase that "all men are created equal," was continually caught between the logic of his own position and the realities of American society. When Jefferson retired to the palatial surroundings of Monticello to be attended by a retinue of slaves, he said he hoped that the way was being prepared, "under the auspices of Heaven, for a total emancipation." Later, during the controversy over the admission of Missouri, he mused that Americans had a "wolf by the ears, and we can neither hold him, nor safely let him go. Justice is in one scale and self-preservation in the other."[1]

The classic statement of the value conflict at the heart of the racial dilemma of America is that of Myrdal.

> The "American Dilemma" . . . is the ever-raging conflict between, on the one hand, the valuations . . . which we shall call the "American Creed," where the American thinks, talks, and acts under the influence of high national and Christian precepts, and, on the other hand, the valuations . . . of individual and group living, where personal and local interests; economic, social and sexual jealousies; considerations of community prestige and conformity; group prejudice against particular types of people; and all sorts of miscellaneous wants, impulses, and habits dominate his outlook.[2]

In this chapter we shall look at these dilemmas, not as theoretical issues, but in very personal terms. These dilemmas (and others) came to light in our interviews with ministers and lay persons of both races in all parts of the country. We could not help being impressed with the very difficult personal decisions and sacrifices required of virtually every person in racially transitional communities.

The names of the persons and churches have been changed, but the stories are actual incidents as told to us by the participants.

Dilemmas of White Ministers

Craig Butler is a soft-spoken but articulate white minister. In the late 60s he became pastor of a congregation in a racially changing community.

Butler, though a man of few words, is a social activist; he would be described as liberal. He had worked in the area of human relations, especially race relations, for some years.

Butler's church was located in a close-in suburb of a large industrial city in the Midwest. That city experienced the trauma of urban unrest, decay, and financial deterioration so characteristic of many major cities during the 60s.

The area around the church contained modest middle-class housing, attractively designed, with a wide variety of services. By most standards it was a desirable place to live. The community experienced rapid racial change, but without drastic deterioration or a major cutback of city services. By and large, the homes were purchased by persons much like those who first occupied them—middle class—with one difference: The new families were black.

Because of the rapid racial change, the community had to deal with many issues at the same time—quality education, student relations, rapid housing turnover, police/community relations. Craig Butler emerged as a central figure. His instincts concerning human relations and his commitment to social justice placed him at the heart of things. He was involved in key meetings and discussions regarding the future of the community.

Butler's church, Mt. Hope, became an important meeting place for many major community gatherings. Some of his members felt uncomfortable about his prominent role and the new reputation of Mt. Hope as a focal point for the community, but Craig enjoyed a measure of support that allowed him to be both community leader and local pastor.

Black adults and youth began attending Mt. Hope Church in sizeable numbers. Generally, they were well received, but most already knew Butler, at least by reputation, and many had already attended community meetings there.

As community transition progressed, white residents continued to leave the community, and they also left Mt. Hope. But new black families became a part of the community and of the church. These new families took leadership roles, assumed financial support, and were involved in the community.

Butler was not without his dilemmas: How to relate to white members opposed to community involvement? How to attract the newcomers without patronizing them? How and when to alter the worship and program to reflect the interests and needs of the new constituency in the congregation? Could a white minister really preach to, and be the pastor of, an increasingly black congregation?

But Butler was able to work through his frustrations. His sensitive leadership, compassion, and commitment made it possible for him to lead his congregation through the racial transition, and he became the white pastor of a predominantly black church in a predominantly black community. Craig's story was an exception to the typical situation we observed.

Perhaps no form of ministry has proved as frustrating and confusing for white clergy as serving in a racially changing community. Ten or more years ago, when white ministers found themselves in the midst of racial change, there seemed to be basically only two options open to them. They could ignore the racial change and concentrate on maintaining a viable white congregation; or they could lead the congregation in accepting the challenge to become an "integrated" congregation.

When we visited local churches across the nation and interviewed ministers and lay people of different denominations, certain issues faced by white ministers seemed to be similar, whether the congregations were in the South, North, East, or West. Only those issues that came to our attention most often will be treated here.

1. Why Am I Here?

Much to our regret, we met ministers who had little or no commitment to a ministry in a racially changing community. As we listened to them, it was evident that they would leave as soon as the opportunity presented itself. We are not addressing ourselves to this situation directly, but we would like to say, in passing, that those denominational leaders responsible for assigning pastors to congregations, and those local church leaders who have the responsibility to "call" new pastors, need to be more sensitive to the specialized nature of ministry required in racially changing communities.

Ministers are not entirely different from other professionals. They want to succeed. They are concerned that future opportunities will be influenced by how well they do in their present assignment. Some ministers are so anxious to make a "success" of their situation that they are reluctant to share with denominational leadership any knowledge of just how bad the situation really is. This may preserve their image, but it also may cut them off from the possibility of needed emotional support.

Too many ministers felt they were being left to handle their frustrations all alone, and that these frustrations were adversely affecting their personal and family lives. It was not uncommon to uncover feelings of pessimism and hopelessness so pervasive that they had affected a spouse or children in the family.

As the neighborhood begins to shift from predominantly white to predominantly black, the possibilities for interracial contacts multiply. For some ministers this interracial community is a brand new experience. They may have had few contacts across racial lines. This may be true for the minister's family, as well.

In many instances, the pastor and family watch their white neighbors move away and find they are the only white family left on the block. Sometimes the minister's children are among the few white children remaining in the school. Two questions raised most frequently by white ministers are: Should the parsonage be moved? Should we place our children in a private school?

The matter of schools becomes crucial to the family in the racially changing community. One minister became more and more dissatisfied with the schools and finally enrolled his children in a private school. When we asked him how he felt, he said, "I do not feel professionally obligated to have my child attend school in our neighborhood if I view the school as inferior. Especially if I feel that improvement cannot take place until after my child has left school." In most instances the minister has had a high commitment to public education. And now, in a sense, to give up on public education is a hard pill to swallow. Families are greatly concerned about this issue.

Even if the quality of education in the school does not decrease significantly, the children may be faced with anti-white attitudes in a few black students. The parents again have to struggle with the question, Should we remove our children from the school? Regardless of the answer, this problem produces a degree of defeat and pain for a family committed to public education and integration. One minister reported that his wife "forced" him to withdraw their children from the schools. Another pastor said hopelessly, "In this area, those who can afford to—Black and White—send their children to private schools."

For the parent, education is perhaps the most important ingredient in the development and nurture of their children. The schools therefore are critical institutions in the life of any community. Whites who find themselves in a community where the schools are in questionable condition may have many more options than nonwhites. Those who can afford to do so will send their children to private schools; others, who are able, will move! In an article by Ray C. Rist of the National Institute of Education, it is stated, "It can be said, unequivocally, that the major unresolved issue facing American education remains: How to significantly improve the education of minority and poor children."[3]

If this fact is accepted, then white ministers located in communities that are now becoming predominantly minority communities will continue to be plagued by this question. It should be clear, however, that the difficulty is one faced by black pastors and their families, as well. For the white pastor, however, it does have peculiar implications. The white pastor is likely to be more severely criticized for sending his or her children to school outside the neighborhood. Many will see this as symbolizing a lack of willingness to identify with the community.

The location of the parsonage is a similar personal dilemma faced by the white minister in the racially changing community. The family may genuinely feel that it does not want to be a white minority in a predominantly black community. Even when there is no particular threat, such as increasing crime or hostility, some ministers have struggled with this question. For some others, the question is most critical when the children reach dating age and it becomes apparent that there are few other white youth in the community.

To be committed to an integrated community and to attempt to develop an integrated congregation while the pastor's family lives in an all-white community, presents a strange dichotomy! Most ministers know this—the sensitive ones agonize over it.

2. Can a White Minister Be a Pastor to Black Members?

We met one white minister in the South who was especially effective in relating to the new black residents. Because of his strong pastoral style, he had been able to bring a significant number of black persons into the membership of the church. He admitted, however, that he always questioned whether he could really be a pastor to black people. He said he had heard so much about "the style and effectiveness of black preaching" that he had become more insecure about his preaching than ever before in his ministry.

Other white ministers, sensitive to the need for black leadership, doubted whether they should still be serving a congregation that is becoming predominantly black and ultimately may well become completely black. Their commitment to minority empowerment and their recognition of the importance of black leadership produced a kind of ambivalence. On the one hand, they may be experiencing some success and satisfaction in the integrated congregation, but on the other, as one white minister wondered, "Might I not be more effective in the white community?"

In the southwestern part of the United States, a white pastor serving a predominantly white church in a predominantly black community witnessed a growing number of black congregations all around the church he was serving. He questioned whether his presence as a white pastor was preventing a more effective outreach to the emerging black community. While neighboring black congregations flourished, his church had only a few black members, after several years of attempting to reach out to the new community.

Another white minister wondered whether his black members would really "open up" to him, or whether some of their pastoral needs were going unmet because they did not have a black pastor with whom they could relate in a more intimate way.

While many white ministers are committed to serving the church in a racially mixed community, few have been able to work through to their satisfaction the question of the relationship of a white pastor to black parishioners. And many still wonder, Should I be here? Even after settling the question of their presence in the changing community, some white pastors were in a quandary as to how aggressive they should be in evangelizing among black prospects. One minister admitted he felt he had no right to "take black members from black churches that need their leadership." Another white minister reported that he had been told by a black pastor in unmistakable terms that he had no right to invite black people into a fellowship "where they are not really wanted in the first place."

Another minister who had been able to attract black members pondered about how he should relate to them; he wasn't sure what style of leadership was appropriate. He didn't want to be too assertive, lest they feel he was patronizing them; yet he didn't want to be so aloof that they might feel he was ignoring them.

One white pastor in a very large church whose members were basically middle-income black families was at a loss as to how to involve these members more effectively. "I would really like to be tougher with them," he said, "but I am afraid they would resent it because I am white." These illustrations of uncertainty are basically a part of the more persistent question of the white minister in the transitional community, Should I be here at all?

3. Integrated or Black?

Many pastors serving congregations in racially changing communities are deeply committed to an integrated church and to the goal of an integrated community. Some have joined with the community in efforts to stabilize it. One pastor lamented, "I don't want to see the community become entirely black." At the same time, these pastors are committed to an open community and freedom of movement for black persons. They would oppose any quotas, but sometimes wonder if any other method will be effective in assuring long-term residential integration.

The white pastor may become even more confused when he or she hears the urgent emphasis being placed on the "ethnic congregation." Do not such efforts threaten the ministry they have been assigned to develop—an integrated congregation? Are their efforts at cross-purposes? Is their ministry hampering the development of ethnic congregations? What is the meaning of the integrated congregation, the ethnic congregation, pluralism, and inclusiveness? These questions nag at those who are attempting to develop ministries in racially changing communities.

The matter is further confused because few denominations have clarified or developed a rationale for the integrated church, or for the development of ethnic congregations. Today both are being espoused, but the white minister often feels caught in the middle.

4. Does Anybody Care?

In many respects, being the white minister in the racially changing community is a lonely existence. Many white colleagues who are serving churches in racially stable communities are unaware of the frustrations of their friends in changing communities. Our observation is that today there are not as many groups of pastors organized for mutual sharing and support as there were ten years ago. Many white pastors feel cut off from their colleagues, both black and white. One minister complained, "Nobody really cares what I'm going through here." And in some instances, black pastors have resented the white pastor who attempted to develop a ministry to and with the black community.

Finally, the most debilitating and destructive influence often confronted by the white pastor is the resistance of the white congregation. A multiplicity of staggering problems confronts the minister in a racially changing community. When, in addition, he or she must face a congregation or local church leadership committed to "keeping them out," the situation becomes overwhelming. One minister's wife was in tears as she described the cruelty her husband suffered from congregational leaders. "Nobody cares," she wept.

5. *What Do I Do About the Residual White Congregation?*

Perhaps the most frequent question we heard was, How do I minister to the residual white congregation? Most of the churches located in racially changing communities are congregations of diminishing membership. The finances are on the decline. Often the buildings are mammoth in size and a burden to maintain. The average age represented in the church is often over sixty. Typically, the Sunday school no longer contains children or youth. We learned of one young adult class—still the strongest class in the Sunday school—attended by those "young adults" who joined the class forty years ago!

The white pastor with a congregation of older members—retirees and shut-ins—is faced with the major task of ministering to this group and reaching out to the community at the same time.

The members of the emerging community are likely to be

much younger than the people of the congregation; the newcomers typically consist mostly of couples with young children.

A pastor looks at the community and soon recognizes that if the congregation is to have a future, it must be with this new community. Yet more and more of the pastor's time may be required to visit the sick, call in the homes of the senior citizens, and meet with a never-ending number of groups in the congregation. The pastor reasons that all these are important functions. But how much time should these responsibilities require? How much time should be devoted to cultivating the new community and reaching potential members?

Some pastors we interviewed had literally given all their time to the dwindling white congregation, virtually ignoring the community. Others had given all their time to the emerging community, ignoring the existing congregation. Most were somewhere in the middle, not really sure how much of their energy ought to be expended in the congregation and how much in the community.

Dilemmas of White Lay Persons

The Winstons, a white couple in their sixties, were members of St. John's Church. They loved their church located in this growing southern city. Their house long ago had become their home. It was the place that held fond memories for them—family and friends had gathered there for many special occasions over the years. They knew their neighbors well. The community institutions—school, local meeting places, commercial establishments—were familiar, but things were changing.

They began to notice a gradual movement of the younger families further out of the city into the suburbs. First they observed the departure of a few of their neighbors. Then they noticed what was happening in the church: there were fewer children, fewer young adults. With each death, with each transfer of a friend to another church, the loss was felt more keenly. New members seemed to be joining the church in diminishing numbers.

Black families were moving onto their street, and the next, and the next. For Sale signs semed to be everywhere. They were becoming a double minority—older and white. Not only were fewer white families to be found in the community, but the streets were bustling with little children, teen-agers "hanging out" on the corners, and young couples holding hands.

But St. John's did not reflect the new vitality present in the community: Few children attended the Sunday school; the youth group no longer existed; there were no longer any young couples. For the Winstons, St. John's was becoming a rather sad place. More and more of the people they knew were leaving—retiring and moving to Florida or joining congregations in the suburbs. The choir, once the pride of the church, now had only a few members.

The neighborhood was changing; the church was changing. The Winstons were getting older. Should they move? Could they afford to, this late in life? St. John's Church meant much to them. Could another church have as much meaning?

The denominational leadership had been concerned about the situation at St. John's for some time. They proposed a possible solution: St. Andrews, a black congregation of the same denomination, had a moderate-sized membership, and an active congregation. It needed a better building. Why not merge the two congregations?

Many of the members of St. John's Church were disturbed by this proposal. Some left. The few remaining believed the merger was not a good idea. "Colored people should have their own church," some suggested. "It just won't work," others said. "This suggestion will chase all the white people away." Many reasons were put forward in opposition to the combining of the two churches.

Nevertheless, the decision was made to merge St. John's and St. Andrew's. The pastor of St. Andrew's Church (a Black) would be the new minister. This was the final straw for most of the remaining members of St. John's. They left.

The Winstons had many questions. They had never known a situation where black and white people were together in the same church. What about the way black people worship? How would that work out? With so few white people remaining, how would they be accepted? But something inside them kept saying, "Maybe we should remain."

The time came for the first worship service of the merged congregations. It was to be a new experience for both the black and the white members. No one really knew what to expect. There were only a handful of white members present for the service. The Winstons were there, and they stayed. When we talked with them, they were the only white members left. With a touch of sadness they said, "Our friends never gave themselves a chance to see if they would like our new church."

The white people we interviewed—factory workers, professionals, housewives, retirees—represented a cross section of the population, as well as a variety of degrees of Christian commitment. By no means were all the people we talked to supportive of racial integration. A few were hostile, some uncertain, others felt trapped, still others were just old and tired. The one thing that became clear to us was how unprepared most of them were to deal adequately and constructively with racial change.

The church, with all its resources, and with all its words about commitment and faithfulness, has not been able to provide sufficient understanding of the gospel to arm the people to fight and eradicate racism. For the most part, when white Christians have been faced with situations in which racism and their Christian faith were put to the test, racism has won.

One active laywoman in a border-state city, whose congregation began to change racially nearly fifteen years ago, is still a member of that same church. Fewer than twelve active white members remain. She lamented, "If only so many of them [the white members] had not left so suddenly, our church would be in a different situation."

In talking to white lay persons, we learned as much about those who had left the church as we did about those who remained. Like their black lay counterparts, these remaining white lay persons often felt abandoned, betrayed, and confused. Most of those who remained were not especially "liberal." In fact, many of the liberal young adults were the first to leave! Also, persons we talked to seemed rather surprised to discover that the church members who were the most "religious" either were among those who left first or provided the greatest resistance to the church's outreach to the new community. "I was surprised to learn how prejudiced Mr. Jones is; he had been one of the strong spiritual leaders of our church," said one woman.

The lay persons who remained included both liberals and conservatives. They were simply "left behind." Some had such an emotional investment in their home or local church that they could not leave; some remained intentionally. But nearly all said that if people had not left and had given the church a chance, they believed the situation would be better.

In a few instances—only a few—some complained that the pastor did not provide adequate leadership. Both extremes were expressed in this regard: Some pastors were too aggressive, too insensitive; others were too passive and so sensitive to their members' feelings that they provided no leadership and did not help the congregation grow.

Many of the people were highly critical of the denominational structure and leadership. One layman who is an employee of the city government in a large southern city, complained, "Our conference has no strategy. They [the city] know what projections to make, but our church leaders don't plan properly."

Another criticized, "Our bishop just doesn't care about these inner-city churches." "There is no overall strategy," agreed a group of white lay persons. "Each church is left to do its own thing."

In a West Coast suburb, a white laywoman involved in the school system said, "If we could begin to work early enough, we could make a difference. Most of the time we spend our energies convincing ourselves it [racial change] won't happen here. The church needs to help us look realistically at our future."

Most of the churches we visited were receiving some kind of mission aid. A number of churches were being supported heavily by denominational assistance. Most of the people were preoccupied with finances. "We aren't even sure we can pay our heat bill." Another group felt especially embarrassed because they couldn't pay their preacher's salary. Some expressed a feeling of being "second class." One angry layman resented being treated "like we were welfare recipients."

The white lay persons who remain in the church in the racially changing community have often been described as unprepared to deal with the future—as resistant, irrelevant, rarely courageous. We did, however, meet some who could be described as courageous: They had remained in congregations in spite of opposition from their friends who had left, and against the wishes of members of their own families. Some who had moved, continued to drive back "because we want our children to have an integrated experience." One of the few middle-aged couples we met continues to be involved—they are the only white family with children still active in their church, which is now 95 percent black.

The white lay persons seemed to be asking three questions:

1. Will the Denomination Help Us?

In nearly every instance when we inquired how helpful the denomination had been in providing assistance in facing the future, there was an overwhelming sense that not enough assistance had been provided. Even though most of the congregations were being supported financially from denominational sources, the lay persons reported that what they needed was guidance earlier, rather than finances later. Some insisted that denominational leaders should have been "tougher with us." Somehow the people expected the denominational leadership to know what the future would hold—and to exercise their authority to help the church face that future.

2. How Can We Stay When the Schools Are in Trouble?

In talking to lay persons in the South and in the North, we heard the same comment. "Younger couples with children were the first to leave." When the neighborhood schools began to decline in quality, when discipline became more and more of a problem, and the quality of the educational program diminished, white parents moved. Many white parents who had moved out of the area but had remained in the church said, "We would still be in the community if it were not for the schools."

One school principal we interviewed argued that white parents are more concerned about the schools "than they are about property values." Interestingly, few of the congregations had been involved in any significant way in maintaining quality education in the community schools.

3. Will We Ever Feel Safe Again?

One factor that seemed to emerge frequently in our discussion with white lay people was their concern with the increase in crime in the community. Whether their fear is real or imagined, when white persons perceive their community as no longer safe, or as not as safe as it once was, they begin to look for other options.

The detailed stories of purse snatchings and muggings of church members or neighbors became so familiar to us that we anticipated them in each city, and we were not disappointed. Loyalty to the congregation and even commitment to an interracial fellowship soon give way to consideration for one's personal safety—or for the safety of one's family.

Persons who are unaccustomed to taking the necessary precautions that seem to go with much of urban living, such as extra locks on the door, outside floodlights, a watchdog, installation of a burglar alarm system, protective window bars, and so forth, soon give up, and conclude that they would rather switch than fight! It becomes difficult—nearly impossible, in fact—to persuade persons to remain in communities where they believe their personal safety is at stake, especially if they have options—and most white people have options.

If ever there was any doubt about the need for churches to become involved in community stabilization, it should be removed after observing the nature of community change in America. The need for local church involvement in the political process, in community organization, in economic and community development, is critical, if there is to be any significant improvement in the manner in which this change takes place.

Dilemmas of Black Ministers

The dilemmas facing the black minister in the transitional community can be illustrated by one pastor whom we interviewed. Let's call him The Reverend William Hamilton. The Reverend Hamilton became the first black pastor of what we will call Christ Church. Historic Christ Church is located in a major metropolitan area of a border state. The black population has increased significantly over the past ten years, and portions of the city's residential area have been experiencing racial change.

Christ Church, located in an area once occupied by upper-middle-class white families, on a major boulevard, attracted worshipers from far and near. It was famous for its cathedral-like sanctuary, beautiful stained-glass windows, high-liturgical worship service, and outstanding music. It is said to have had one of the finest pipe organs in the area. Christ Church still has paid soloists.

In the mid-1950s the neighborhood began to change from white to black. The 1960s saw an acceleration of this change, so that by the time William Hamilton arrived, the neighborhood was all black. In less than twenty years it has experienced not only racial change, but economic change, as well. The community surrounding Christ Church is now black, but it is changing again, this time from black middle income to black lower income.

When Hamilton was appointed pastor, the membership of Christ Church was still essentially white. The congregation, or at least its leadership, believed that it was time for a black pastor. They had witnessed their membership decreasing from over one thousand to approximately four hundred. Attendance had fallen off to about two hundred. The young adults and younger parents were gone.

The new black minister is articulate, personable, a capable administrator, a conscientious pastor, and an outstanding preacher. Among his black colleagues he is also known as a "whooper" (one who can preach effectively in the black idiom and style).

When we visited the city and met Hamilton, he reported having received approximately 125 new members, most of whom were black. The Sunday morning attendance was then about 50 percent black. A core of white members remained loyal to the church and supportive of the pastor's leadership.

The major problem facing the church is the transfer of leadership from Whites to Blacks. The white members are anxious to release positions of leadership, but the black members, for a number of reasons, are reluctant to accept. Like most new members in any congregation, they are not yet heavily involved in the leadership and financial support of Christ Church. Such commitments come with time. And for a congregation in a transitional situation, time is crucial!

The personal dilemmas of the black pastor in a white congregation are many. Like the white pastor in a racially changing community, he often feels he is alone and lacking a supportive community.

1. How Can I Affirm the Black Experience in a White Congregation?

For most black pastors appointed to a white church in a changing community, the question of maintaining their ethnicity, or blackness, is a fundamental issue. Often such pastors feel guilty because they are not in a black congregation. They may appear to the black community as "Uncle Toms," or at least as "oreos" (black on the outside, but white on the inside). They may be viewed somewhat suspiciously, or with contempt, by other black pastors.

The issue of ethnicity may be most dramatically confronted in the worship service and in the minister's identification with the black community. The black minister finds himself in a quandary as he seeks to be true to the black religious experience, while at the same time relating to the white religious heritage.

Worship is the central focus for all black religious experience. Worship is the ultimate drama, where all of life is relived—sadness, despair, joy, and hope. It is truly Good Friday and Easter, Crucifixion and Resurrection, every week in the black church. Black people talk, not about "going to church," but about "*having* church." The black religious experience is, most of all, an emotional experience. The worship is expected to make one *feel* something, not just hear something.

In a great many white churches worship is more likely to be subdued, with minimal congregational participation and little emotional involvement.

Gilbert H. Caldwell shares an incident which took place in a *white* church in Washington, D.C. While the minister was preaching a sermon, "a lady in the congregation held up various cards." Afterward, he discovered they bore words such as Amen! Go, man, go! and Hallelujah! She came up to him and said, "I often feel deeply moved during the service and would like to shout out my joy. Knowing that you don't do that in a worship service, I had a set of cards printed. When I feel the Spirit move me, I find the right card and hold it up. I know it sounds crazy, but it makes me feel better."[4]

This incident illustrates the restraint that is all too typical of white worship. There is "something" that happens in black worship that does not often happen in white worship.

One of the things that "happens" in a black worship service is the music. Even "white" hymns are sung differently in a black church. But the black gospel music is different! To be sure, there is white gospel music, but the difference between the two is like the difference between George Beverly Shea and James Cleveland.

The black pastor in the white congregation may run into resistance as he or she seeks to incorporate black music and black preaching into the worship service. At Christ Church, William Hamilton was aware of this resistance. He knew that there was not much he could do with the choir, which was an institution in itself. So he persuaded one of the black musicians to organize a youth choir and a children's choir. Both were composed only of black children, for by this time there were no white children or youth left in the church. These two choirs sang spirituals. Occasionally the youth choir would sing one of the more sophisticated gospel numbers. Later the minister began to bring in black soloists, who would sing just before he delivered his sermon. These songs were often familiar ones in the black tradition. His preaching style had elements familiar to both races in the congregation. He didn't "whoop," but you would often hear black worshipers commenting on how " 'hard' Reverend Hamilton preached today."

When we asked the pastor how he was able to handle the contrasts between the black religious experience and the white religious heritage, he commented, "The preacher must be secure within. I don't feel the need to prove myself. But I did make changes." He seemed clear about his goals and objectives. He did not make changes willy-nilly; he had a timetable for changes in the worship service and in the church program.

In fact, the pastor was able to maintain the highly liturgical ritual that he had found when he arrived. He commented, "When you have a good history, you can bring in new elements without destroying that good history." He knew that many of the white worshipers traveled many miles because they loved the formal worship service. He reasoned that if they returned because of their appreciation and need for that liturgy, he would not alter it without careful consideration. Instead, he attempted to provide ingredients of *both* black and white tradition. The worship service became a blending of high-liturgical ritual, embellished with unmistakable "soul."

In another of our interviews in a different city, the black pastor of a predominantly white congregation with a high-liturgical tradition had a serious confrontation over the use of black gospel music. The pastor believed that if the church was going to have any impact on *that* community, the music and the worship service would have to change. But both the white and the black members seriously objected to the use of black gospel music. One black member vehemently declared, "If I had wanted to be a Baptist, I would have joined a Baptist church."

The style of worship service will continue to be one of crucial issues facing the church in the racially transitional community. The dilemma of the black minister is, How quickly should the black religious experience be incorporated into what has been a white-oriented worship service?

2. *How Does a White Congregation Minister to a Black Community?*

A second serious problem for the black minister is the desire to minister to the black community while recognizing the responsibility to be a pastor to a white congregation. Our observation in most of the cities we visited is that, for the most part, the black ministers appointed to congregations in racially changing communities are newly or recently out of seminary. They are activist and deeply committed to "the Black liberation struggle." They want to be, and often are, involved in community issues and organizations, and are addressing themselves to "challenging and changing the system."

The residual white congregation is made up mainly of older members, who are perhaps more in need of pastoral care now than ever before in their church life. These white members have seen their friends and family die. Their old neighbors have moved away. The community institutions which once were stablizing forces in their lives—the corner grocer or druggist, the familiar newsstand, the neighborhood restaurant—are all gone now.

These loyal, sometimes bigoted, often frightened, white members remain. Their pastor is now young, black, and activist. Hospital visits and pastoral calls to relive the past are not likely to be high on such a pastor's agenda. Maintaining the rituals and "monuments" of the white residual congregation may not seem very important.

The black pastor will be challenged by the call to join in the liberation struggle, but also will be reminded of the call to tend the flock. One such minister confessed, "I just can't forget that those old white people are God's children, too. I just can't forget that." Torn by the need to be involved in the struggle as well as to be pastor to those who may not be aware of, or even care about, that struggle, is an awesome problem for the black minister. For it is not only a question of ministry, but a test of ethnicity.

> The black church person and the black local church in a white structure must possess a number of traits to be active, effective, and true to what God has done through and in the black experience. He or she must be able to cope with the white establishment while at the same time maintaining contact and emotional ties and involvement in the Black Liberation Struggle. A dual kind of existence is required of those who would be a part of white institutions and at the same time be responsive to the Black Experience.[5]

While a few of the black pastors we talked to had worked through this dilemma, it became increasingly clear that few lay members of the congregations, and not very many white administrators, were even aware that the struggle was going on.

3. How Can I Build a New Black Church While Pastor to a White Congregation?

A third concern for the black pastor in a predominantly white church in the racially changing community is ministry to the white congregation. This problem is different from that in number 2, in that it is not related to the pastor's involvement in the Black liberation struggle; it is not one of compulsion to be a pastor to white people. Rather, it results from the clear understanding that a new community is emerging and that that community needs a church. The pastor must establish a black congregation—and fast. Every digression from working toward that goal is time lost.

The reality of the situation may suggest that there is little time or possibility for a transitional integrated congregation. If the minister does not act quickly, creatively, and responsibly as the white people leave, he may be left with an empty building. Questions rush in on the pastor: How to concentrate time and effort toward the communty, meanwhile providing necessary ministry to the congregation? Can the minister justify ignoring those who pay the bills while being involved in the community and reaching out to new black people in the area? What is the appropriate balance?

The elderly, diminishing, white congregation and its needs may be a barrier to the attraction of vigorous, enthusiastic, young black families. One dedicated older white layman said, "If I was a black father with children, I wouldn't come to this church!" When questioned further, he elaborated, "There are no young people, no Sunday school, and our worship service is dead—why would black people want to come to our church anyway?"

One minister admitted that he thought he would be "better off if all the white people left." Another took the opposite position. "I want my people to love me. If they love me, I can handle the rest." His strategy was to be a responsive pastor to the handful of whites, but to maintain an aggressive, evangelistic outreach to the black community. When his efforts in the community made it impossible for him to perform some particular congregational duty, he theorized, his people would understand.

4. How Can I Reconcile Conflicting and Unrealistic Expectations?

A fourth dilemma faced by the black pastor in the transitional community is the conflicting and unrealistic expectations held by a variety of persons, both within and outside the congregation.

Several years ago, extensive studies were made of the "crisis in the ministry." These studies were conducted because of the high incidence of emotional problems in, and dropouts from, the parish ministry. Further, there was great dissatisfaction among the laity and a growing gap between the clergy and the laity. The studies revealed that a major source of frustration experienced by both pastors and lay people was that they held conflicting and contradictory expectations for the role of the pastor.

Edgar Mills suggested that there are three categories of clergy role conflicts: (a) conflicts involving external obligations (such as those of the minister who is "caught in a crossfire of the essential bureaucratic norms of his superiors, the professional norms of his peers, and the popular norms of his lay clientele"); (b) conflicts between his own internalized norms and the pressures of external situations (such as the conflicts between the tasks a minister considers essential, and the many unimportant things that preempt his time); and (c) conflicts resulting from his own internalized values and expectations that are mutually incompatible.[6]

In addition, there is the problem of role flexibility. As the minister moves through the course of a work day, he or she encounters a variety of situations, each with its own expectations and each requiring different leadership styles. "At times, his effectiveness depends upon his being authoritative and directive. At other times he must be highly permissive and responsive to delicate nuances of feeling. He must understand group processes and effective styles of intervention to bring about change."[7]

Joseph Fichter described the urban ministry succinctly. "The present dynamic situation in the urban American parish seems to require not so much the emphasis on one role more than another, as a simultaneous coordination of multiple roles."[8]

In our interviews, one question we never failed to ask was, What do the officials of your denomination expect of you as the pastor here? Nearly all the white pastors responded that they had received no special instructions. On the other hand, when black pastors were asked the same question, they responded with clarity: They were expected to build a new black congregation. Usually, by the time the black pastor arrived, it was clear that a new congregation was needed. They were expected to build up the membership, increase the Sunday morning worship attendance, and develop youth and Sunday school programs. In contrast, the white pastors tended to be oriented to the residual white congregation. They were not expected to build *black* membership or attendance. About the only clear expectations of them were to keep the church open and to pay the assessments to the denomination.

All too often, the black pastor is expected to be a miracle worker. It was not uncommon to hear a judicatory executive or lay person say, "All we need is a black pastor." They assume that the black pastor, just by being there, will turn the situation around. It is expected that great throngs of black people will appear "like they do at the colored Baptist church down the street." Not only is it anticipated that the black pastor will perform this miracle, but that he will do it right away. Denominational leaders, as well as parishioners, may have an unrealistic time frame in which they expect a new black congregation to emerge.

The community also has expectations of the black pastor. Racial transition is often a time of disorganization in the community. The community needs all the leadership it can find. The black community has come to expect its preachers to be involved, so the new pastor soon is thrust into the role of community leader. The community expects the minister to represent it at city hall, advocate for it before the welfare agencies, represent its concerns before the police department, meet with the school officials, work with parents, and so on.

If the black pastor is in a denomination or judicatory with few minority members, he or she will be expected to play a prominent role in judicatory and denominational affairs, also. The minister may be assigned to more committees than can be handled responsibly; there is, however, the awareness that failure to attend a meeting or accept membership on a committee may result in no minority presence or participation. Consequently, the black pastor may be expected to attend more meetings out of the parish than does his white counterpart.

In most instances, the local church may be receiving some denominational subsidy. Those who grant these subsidies also have their expectations. Reports and forms must be filled out. Conferences must be attended, training seminars are required, and so on. And frequently the pastor must help raise funds by visiting other local churches, speaking at women's meetings and youth groups, "to tell the story of our church."

There is growing concern in business and industry about the kind of stress placed upon black professionals working in white structures. The high expectations for performance of these people—often conflicting and unrealistic—are taking their toll. William B. Sapp, a neuropsychiatrist from Atlanta, refers to the mental anguish Blacks suffer at the hands of insensitive white employers in large corporations as the "Black syndrome." He observes, "Young Blacks trapped in well-paying but psychologically shattering jobs are better off quitting."[9]

There are parallels in the church. The conflicting and often unrealistic expectations, combined with the tensions of ministry in transitional communities, may take their toll on the ministers. Greater responsibility should be assumed by denominational officials for becoming acquainted with the personal dilemmas that may be experienced by these ministers. Opportunities for renewal should be provided. More extensive resources must be developed to help support pastors in these high-stress ministries.

Dilemmas of Black Lay Persons

Mr. James Taylor is a black layman. He is an extremely dedicated church worker and a conscientious father and husband. About fifteen years ago, Mr. Taylor moved his family out of the overcrowded black section of one of the major cities in the Midwest. The family moved to a middle-income white community. The Taylor family was one of the first black families to move into that section of Smithdale.

Smithdale was a lovely community—tree-lined streets, nice lawns, well-kept homes, and good schools. The Taylors had found their dream house and their ideal community. Yet there was some anxiety, for they were doubtful about their reception from their white neighbors—they expected the worst! But their fears were not realized: They were not harrassed; they were simply ignored! "As time went on," Mrs. Taylor said, "the neighbors warmed to us, and we soon made friends and had no problems on our street."

Other black families followed the Taylors, not in great numbers, but at a steady rate. Mr. Taylor was a member of a black congregation in another part of the city but finally decided to attend a church in his new community. The Taylors sought out the nearest church of their denomination and attended the worship service there. The neighborhood was well integrated by this time, but the neighborhood church they visited was essentially white—there were possibly two black families in the church. The Taylors were well received and eventually joined the Smithdale church. They became very active—the children in the church school programs and Mr. and Mrs. Taylor in a variety of activities within the church.

Soon they began to notice that more and more of their neighbors were leaving—moving away. Often, they didn't even say goodbye—the next day they were simply gone. The same pattern was followed in the Smithdale church. People would leave for summer vacation and not return. Soon the church school dwindled, but Mr. Taylor observed that new black children were beginning to attend.

One hot summer day a riot erupted not far from Smithdale. Soon thereafter, Whites moved out *en masse*—they left the community; they left the church. The Taylors were disillusioned and disappointed.

Most of the black lay persons we interviewed were those who were among the "first Negroes to come to this church." It appeared from our interviews that the first black members of the predominantly white congregations were persons who had been members of black congregations of that denomination before moving to the new community.

When asked why they chose an all-white congregation, most answered, "Because it was closest to where I lived." Many of these persons had moved into the community when it was still predominantly white. They were essentially committed to an integrated church, and were disturbed that many or most of the white people were leaving. Some black lay persons described, with some degree of pain, how difficult it had been to feel welcome in the all-white congregation, "But I kept coming anyway."

One father was particularly impressed with the educational building and the organization of the church school. "I finally saw a Sunday school with ample materials and resources."

One black woman in a midwestern community was obviously hostile towards "black worship." She said, "I was glad to find a church where there wasn't a lot of hollering going on!" When we talked to her and her white pastor about the possibility of making the worship services more attractive to the community, now over 90 percent black, she replied, "If you start that gospel music mess, I will become a Catholic."

We believe it is fair to say that many of the congregations we visited had been able to attract only a very few black members. Some of these churches had black members who had been in the church for four or five years. One church had a small group of black people who had been members for nearly ten years. The black members, however, represented only a small percentage of the membership. Even as more and more Whites left the community and the church, the black membership did not grow substantially. One white pastor said, "We have black people visiting nearly every Sunday, but they don't come back." Another said, "The black people who do come to our worship service never come on a regular basis. I wish we could get all of them to show up on the same Sunday."

One black woman we talked to was a member of a very prestigious old-line congregation in a large midwestern city. She sang in the choir, served on the local church board, and was involved in other activities. She had been a member for several years, having been attracted to the church because of its excellent music and its educational program for the children. The church is really a metropolitan church, where few of the members actually live in the immediate community. which is predominantly black. The few black members of the church, however, do *not* live in the community. Like the white members, they drive in to historic First Church.

Most of the black persons we talked to were either frustrated or angry. Some even felt betrayed by the white members. They were ambivalent about recruiting more black members. Some were still concerned about the white members who had left; others wanted to know how to attract new white members. Let us examine some of their concerns.

1. Pro-Integration
Nearly all the black members we interviewed wanted to live in an integrated community and to worship at an integrated

church. "I moved to this community because it was predominantly white. If I had known it was going to turn black, I would not have moved here," said one woman bitterly. One man, whose home was now nearly paid for, said, "If I had known this (the community change) was going to happen, I would have moved further out."

After more conversation, we discovered that these persons were not anti-black, not even pro-white, but that they were vigorous supporters of integration.

2. Betrayed by Whites

Second, they had a strong sense that their white neighbors had betrayed them. Few Blacks who had moved into the community when it was largely white reported having any negative experiences. Some reported initial coolness by their neighbors, while others had experienced a very warm reception. All reported good relations with their neighbors, as time went on. Indeed, the neighbors, time and again, had expressed their support for an integrated community.

But eventually, For Sale signs began to appear. Soon their friends and neighbors were avoiding them. One white woman, in tears, confessed to her black friend, "I don't want to go, but Margaret is going to be in high school next year. She will be dating." Some neighbors even "moved out by night." The street became "blacker and blacker." "I wanted my kids to be in an integrated school, but now the school is nearly all black." When asked why they thought "white flight" occurs, they gave an assortment of replies.

"Racism"
"White people can't deal with interracial dating and the possibility of interracial marriage."
"Real estate interests"
"When you get down to it, white people can't accept black people."

"Schools began to deteriorate."

"Children began to experience anti-white expression by the black kids."

"Crime increased."

Whatever the reasons, these black lay persons had dreamed of living in an integrated community. That dream had been shattered, and for the most part, they were bitter. They were also frustrated because they did not feel they were able to move again.

3. Even the "Christians" Ran.

The bitterness expressed about their community was often more pronounced regarding their church. The black persons had believed their churches were committed to integration. One active black layman said, "I saw our church school change from all-white, when I came here, to all-black, now."

One woman said, "If only they had been 'up-front' about it." Apparently few black persons heard any white members say they were leaving the church because of race. One person said, "I dreaded to see summer come, because I knew people would go on vacation and not return."

One man remembered when a black fraternal order worshiped as a group in his church. Apparently, it had been the custom of the group to worship together at one of the local churches, once a year. "After the group came to our church, several white families left."

For the most part, the churches we visited were experiencing membership decline. The church schools were barely organized. Where they were strong, they were more than likely all-black. The parents of the children in the youth programs and Sunday school generally were not members of the church. Most of the young white adults were gone. The remaining white members were older persons. The black members were middle-aged, but there were no white counterparts. The black lay persons were feeling they had been avoided once again.

4. White or Black Worship?

The black persons interviewed were ambivalent regarding a movement toward a black worship style. Even when there were few white people still in the church, some of the black lay persons believed it would be a mistake to try to develop such a service. Some of the white pastors expressed some openness to exploring the possibility, but they said their black members advised them against it.

We did interview some black persons who believed "we should have some black preaching and black music here." However, they weren't sure how it should be introduced or developed. Even those who were supportive of the development of a black worship style believed the white members would not accept it.

Black lay persons who are committed to an integrated congregation may well be in an untenable position, in a racially changing community. They recognize the need for new people to come into the congregation if the local church is to survive; however, they also are aware that the possibility of securing new white members is practically nil. If white members continue to leave, and they are successful at reaching new black members, it means the collapse of their dream—an integrated congregation.

One black woman was very clear about her understanding of the integrated church. For her, the goal is not an integrated church in and of itself, but a serving church. She and others have become frustrated when they recognized the failure of their congregation to reach out more aggressively to the new black residents. These black lay persons say that "not enough is being done to attract the community." One very articulate laywoman was especially critical of her church for being quite open to "serve the community, but not as open to have the community serve in the church." She felt that she was considered too aggressive by her congregation.

One black couple who are very active in their church expressed some guilt because of their belief that their congregation needed a black minister. "We like our pastor," they said, "but we don't think he is able to reach this (black) community. Sunday mornings, he lectures, he doesn't preach."

The laity, like the clergy, experience the frustration and anxiety of the church in the racially changing community. They, like the pastors, have commitment and concern. They, too, need to be equipped to be more effectively involved in this unique and challenging ministry.

Patterns of Transition
in Communities

Most discussions of racial transition have negative connotations of an invasion by undesirable persons and of neighborhood deterioration. Originally, urban sociologists borrowed the term "invasion" from plant ecology, where it referred to one species of plants replacing another. In the context of the neighborhood, however, it probably reflects the value bias of white sociologists as they observed "foreign" elements entering previously stable, homogeneous, white communities.

Our discussion will avoid that language. A term such as "invasion" emphasizes the past residents, as if they have an inalienable right to protect their turf, while the newcomers have no right to "the pursuit of happiness." It seduces one into thinking that stability is normal and that neighborhood homogeneity is the natural state of affairs. It places the blame for neighborhood decline—if it does occur—on the newcomers, ignoring the culpability of absentee landlords, lending institutions, real estate people, and city officials, who facilitate the deterioration in their own ways.

The term "transition" is preferable because it is somewhat less pejorative. It is important to emphasize the emerging community. "Transition" keeps our attention focused on the future, rather than the past—on the new community that is in the process of being established, rather than on the community that is on the wane.

One dictionary defines "transition" as "a movement or passage from one position, state, subject, etc., to another;

change." Its opposite would be a stable equilibrium. The essence of transition is nonequilibrium and instability, with net movement being in only one direction, from one thing to another.

Until fairly recently, community "transition" meant that an area was changing from white to black—a process that was thought to be irreversible. Two variations in patterns of urban change necessitate a broadening of that definition: (a) Sections of some cities are shifting from Anglo to Hispanic or Asian, and (b) many cities have at least some neighborhoods where reverse transition is taking place; they are changing from black to white, or from lower-income to middle- or upper-income, as younger, educated professionals buy and renovate older houses.

Some church groups have broadened the definition of "transition" to mean any type of major change in the community: racial, population increase (suburbanization, conversions, high-rise buildings), population decrease (demolition, highway construction, abandonment), economic (entry of lower- or higher-income persons), age (entry of young adults, senior citizens), life-style (entry of conservatives, "hippies," or Appalachian people), religious increase or decrease (Roman Catholic, Jewish, Protestant), and so on.[1]

While these transitions are important and some of our observations apply to them, our focus is limited to racial transition. Dealing with racial transition inevitably involves facing the racial attitudes of church leaders, the image of the denominations in the minority community, and the role of the church in combating institutional racism (both in its own organizational structures and in society).

The Dynamics of Community Change

Community transition is the result of a profound change along five dimensions: (1) social definition of an area—its "image"; (2) physical condition of the housing and neighborhood facilities (such as parks, sidewalks, street lights); (3) life cycle of the population of the area; (4) socio-economic status of the residents; and (5) community dominance.

1. Social Definition

Communities have more or less recognizable boundaries and more or less stable identities. They also have a position in the hierarchy of communities in the metropolitan area. While these identities, boundaries, and images are relatively stable, they do change over time.

The "ghetto" is primarily a social definition placed upon a unit of space: originally, "a section of a city in which, in former times in most European countries, all Jews were required to live; a section predominantly inhabited by Jews." In America, the "ghetto" has come to mean "a section of the city, especially a thickly populated slum, often as a result of social or economic restrictions."

At a collective level, social behavior has been described as "territorial." "Once a slice of physical space is identified as a territorial realm of a specific group, any attempt to alter this assignment results in group conflict, both overt and covert."[2]

Whites have more options concerning where they can live, so it is their behavior that determines how racial transition will take place. If they refuse to sell or move, the area cannot change—as evidenced in some solid, moderate-income, ethnic white communities immediately adjacent to the ghetto.

2. Physical Condition

In every neighborhood, the houses and neighborhood facilities go through a normal, natural, aging process. As they become older, they need more maintenance, and the original equipment requires replacement. Rarely do property owners seem to prepare for the depreciation of their homes. The prices usually do not decline at a regular rate to provide for this depreciation; rather, they may decline suddenly, in response to lack of market confidence. Many older cities are suffering from the obsolescence of large portions of their housing stock.

Racial transition is related to this normal aging process. Older houses tend to be handed down to lower-income groups, but some reach "antique" status and may be reoccupied by upper-income persons (usually whites).

3. Life Cycle of the Residents

There is a natural correlation between the characteristics of the housing units in a neighborhood and the life cycle of the occupying families. Some communities, such as apartment areas, may be more appropriate for singles, for young couples, and for senior citizens. Other neighborhoods were built for families, and tend to go through cycles paralleling the life cycle of the bulk of the residents. They are thriving when occupied by younger families; they tend to lose their vigor as the population ages and the children grow up and leave.

The aging of the population is part of the process that promotes racial transition. Property inevitably comes on the market as people retire or become too old to keep it up. If there is not sufficient demand by one race, the vacated units may become occupied by persons of another race. In part, racial transition represents the recycling of the property from an older to a younger population, and the emerging community may have a vitality similar to that of the same community twenty or thirty years ago.

4. Socio-Economic Status

From a different perspective, racial transition may be seen as merely a particular stage in the larger process of "filtering" or "trickle-down."

When first created, the new neighborhood . . . is initially occupied by households in the upper half of the national income distribution, because lower-income households cannot afford to live there. As time passes, the housing units in this neighborhood become older and less stylish compared to newer units. . . . At the same time, the real income of many households initially living in this neighborhood increases. Many move to even newer housing units that are larger, more stylish, and in "fancier" neighborhoods. . . . Relatively low-income households continually move into the housing in this area. . . .

As more time passes, the once new housing becomes less and less desirable compared to the newest and best in society, even if it is well maintained, because it is occupied by a succession of *relatively* lower and lower income groups with absolutely much lower incomes than those who first lived there. Finally the housing becomes occupied by the lowest income groups in society and falls into complete disrepair.[3]

Charles L. Leven and his associates have criticized early studies for failing to distinguish the impact of race from that of income. They believe that income may be an even more significant factor than race. They propose a theory of "arbitrage" to explain the complex relationships.

Arbitrage is "the successive devaluation of housing by recurring waves of turnover to occupants of lower-income status. . . . As the arbitrage process goes on and adjacent neighborhoods move down this continuum, the worst housing would (eventually) be abandoned. . . .

Change in the racial and income composition of neighborhoods and the successive downgrading of the housing stock as landlords adjust to even lower rental levels . . . the depopulation of neighborhoods and landlords' abandonment of their properties as the dwelling units become simultaneously unlivable and unprofitable.[4]

Note that this analysis describes a process of handing down housing and neighborhoods to successively lower-income groups—not necessarily different racial groups. The two processes may well operate independently.

It is commonly assumed that the economic level of the people drops when minorities enter the community. In many transitional communities, this is *not* the case, since it is the higher-income members of the minority groups who have the economic resources and emotional drive to be the pioneers.

Experience indicates that it is only later that the economic status changes—somtimes many years later. The first transition is racial. The second is economic as, following the "filtering" principle, higher-income members of the minority group are replaced with persons of the same race, but with lower incomes.

In the period of extensive black migration from the South and the tremendous pressure for expansion of the black community, the second (economic) change often took place soon after the first (racial) change. In the 1980s, these two changes will probably be separated by a longer period of time.

5. Community Dominance

By "community dominance" we do not necessarily mean political control, but that the minority group has the dominant influence in the institutions in the community (stores, playgrounds, schools, neighborhood newspapers, etc.) and the cultural patterns of the area. Regardless of who has the *ultimate* control, there comes a time when the minority group's social patterns, leaders, and so on, become dominant in the community.

Most—but not all—transition occurs in older areas adjacent to existing minority areas. The expansion of black communities and the movement of minority persons tend to follow directional patterns laid down by previous newcomer groups, often described as if the black people were a tide engulfing an area. They move along radial lines of transportation, restricted by sociological barriers (rivers, railroads, parks, highways), attracted by neighborhood amenities, and repulsed by strong, well-defined ethnic communities (at least for a time). Those patterns are so well documented that, to a large extent, the neighborhoods that probably will go through racial transition, and the churches that are likely to be affected, can be predicted several years in advance.[5]

Stages of Community Change

Some communities may remain stable and racially mixed for an indefinite period of time. But others go through a process of transition from an all-white to a predominantly black community. Transitional communities seem to go through four stages: (1) pretransition; (2) early transition; (3) late transition; (4) post-transition, or established minority community.

1. Pretransition

A pretransitional neighborhood is one that has the most potential for change. Minorities may not yet have entered, or they may be present in such small numbers as to be "invisible." Their presence is not a factor in the community's self-understanding, its image, or in the real estate market. Just by looking at an area, it might be difficult to distinguish a pretransitional neighborhood from one that is stable and all-white. But the potential is there.

If the primary demand for housing is from minority persons, that community is already in the transitional process, regardless of the numbers or percentages involved. Conversely, a community can be racially stable with almost any percentage of minority persons present—if there is sufficient, continued demand for housing on the part of whites to maintain that percentage at a stable level.

2. Early Transition

This is the stage when most people begin to become aware of the presence of minority persons in a community.

In most cases, community transition is *not* marked by violence or overt white resistance. The first few minority families may be welcomed, or at least not resisted. When we think of the hundreds of communities that have changed over the last thirty years, we realize how few nasty incidents there have been.

There are many persons who will actually welcome minority persons and look forward to the opportunity of living in an integrated neighborhood. In the early-transition stage, race relations may be quite positive. Whites and Blacks—often led by church members—may attempt to maintain a stable, racially mixed community. The more liberal and activist members of the community often mobilize the church, the PTA, and organize neighborhood associations and block clubs to maintain the interracial character of the community.

As more and more black people move into the community and increasing numbers of Whites move out, however, even the least prejudiced Whites conclude that they, too, must leave. For some, racial factors may be less significant than a fear of economic loss in selling their homes. For others, the loss of the familiar community is more than they can take. Many leave reluctantly, forced, they feel, by pressures too overwhelming to resist.

Those who tried so hard to maintain an integrated community find that their dream is not going to be realized. They feel a sense of defeat and reluctantly accept the reality that theirs is a transitional community.

3. Late Transition

The early stage of transition is separated from the late stage by the "tipping point."[6] In the early-transition stage, white people may be aware of the presence of minority persons in the community, but most of them are calm or friendly toward the newcomers. They do not move. But there comes a time when a sufficient number of white persons have decided that the community is becoming or will become dominantly a minority community and that they no longer want to live there. The experience so far is that the maximum out-movement of Whites takes place when the percentage of minorities in the community reaches 20 to 25 percent.[7] But this percentage may change in the 1980s.

It seems likely that, rather than being the result of uncontrollable market forces, the tipping point threshold is crossed when various important institutional decision-makers make choices in the light of what they perceive as the inevitable future. When enough of the community influentials begin to act as if the neighborhood will become a minority community, it becomes a self-fulfilling prophecy.

Expectations about the future of housing values became institutionalized in lending practices called "redlining" and in the real estate selling practice called "racial steering."

Redlining refers to the practice of drawing a line around certain areas and automatically denying mortgages to white buyers, since those areas have been defined as "changing" or "gone." At one time, lending institutions denied that such a practice existed; more recently they have claimed that it is based on "sound business judgment."

Tacit admission that *de facto* redlining is an inherent characteristic of economically sound lending practices is contained in the report of the President's Committee on Urban Housing (1968). The Committee pointed out that for the most of its history, the FHA was required to operate on an actuarily sound basis and that this "compelled FHA to refuse to write mortgage insurance on properties located in risky neighborhoods."[8]

Regardless of whether redlining occurs because of a malicious conspiracy or an institutional insensitivity, the outcome is the same. A shortage of capital for home improvement, rehabilitation, and purchase, contributes to the deterioration of a neighborhood.

Not only are real estate and lending institutions involved, but in several cities, it was reported that the quality of city services, such as street repair, tree trimming, garbage collection, park maintenance, and so on, deteriorated at the time of major racial transition.

The late-transition stage is the time of massive social change. The greatest number of people move out and move in. There is the greatest exchange of property. Subjectively, white people report having lost control of "their" neighborhood institutions.

Just as important as the decline of former neighborhood institutions is the emergence of new community institutions related to the newcomers. Some businesses shift their emphasis and take on new product lines. For example, the bank may emphasize consumer credit, rather than mortgage loans. New types of businesses may move in. Storefront churches may multiply. Individuals may begin to attract the political following that will eventually make them key community leaders.

Community institutions shift their focus and change leadership. These changes do not occur all at once, but are spread out over a period of time. In some places the major changes took place within six to eighteen months; in others, the changes occurred gradually over an eight-to-ten-year period.

4. Post-Transition: Established Minority Community

The post-transitional stage is reached when the minority group becomes the overwhelming numerical majority in the community, and the community leadership changes hands. The post-transitional community is, for all intents and purposes, a *new* community. Sociologically, it is just as new as a suburban subdivision, but its newness is less obvious because the housing is not newly constructed—in the transitional community, only the people are new.

Like other new communities, the post-transitional community can have an excitement, vigor, and status. For a while, it may be the "in" place to live, to have a business, to establish a church. The sociological literature is full of articles on neighborhood "decline," but little has been written about neighborhood "rebirth" with a new—albeit minority—group of residents. For the church, this new community must be its primary concern. It is the future.

Congregations in Transition

Dynamics of Change in Churches

Congregational change tends to follow one of two patterns: (a) gradual change in the racial composition of the congregation, roughly paralleling the transition in the community, or (b) a period of resistance, followed by rapid change or dissolution of the congregation. (The one option that rarely is feasible is to do nothing—yet that is one of the most widely employed strategies.)

Congregational change is not a simple process. It involves changes in a number of areas: (1) relationship to the community; (2) self-image; (3) church program; and leadership (both clergy and lay).

1. Relationship to the Community

As neighborhoods change, community-based institutions are inevitably affected. But is the local church really a community-based institution? One of the common mistakes of church leaders in transitional communities is to believe that it is not. Dozens of closed churches are monuments to organizational decisions based on the erroneous assumption that the local church is somehow immune from the effects of change occurring in the area around the church building.

First of all, let us grant that most Protestant denominations are not organized on a parish basis, in which persons are automatically related to and expected to attend the church in their area. Most Protestant churches draw their members from a wide area. This is especially true for minority congregations, larger churches, congregations from smaller denominations, and congregations which had their roots in an immigrant group.

Ezra Earl Jones has observed that certain types of churches tend to draw their members from a large area: (a) Old First Church (located in the central business district and drawing from the entire city and, in some cases, the metropolitan area); (b) the Metropolitan Regional Church (located at the growing edge of a metropolitan area and accessible to a number of residential neighborhoods); and (c) the Special Purpose Church (organized around one issue or style of ministry, such as a language ministry, charismatic theology, or a chaplaincy to radical young adults).[1]

These are not neighborhood churches. A "neighborhood church" is one that is located in a residential neighborhood in such a way that it is identified with the community around it. Its very name often symbolizes that identification: Norwood Park, Lincoln Avenue, West End. It is fairly obvious that the fate of such a church is tied to the population patterns of the neighborhood. Studies have shown that these churches grow while the community is growing, reach their peak membership at about the time the community reaches its peak population, and later, decline when the population of the community declines.

To a greater extent than is realized, however, the future of other types of churches also is related to their surrounding areas. Many downtown churches are in trouble. Those that are surviving are either drawing new members from the high-rise buildings and redevelopment areas adjacent to the downtown area, or located in smaller cities adjacent to expressways, so that members can get to the church with a minimum of inconvenience.

Metropolitan Regional Churches are not dependent upon any one neighborhood. They can survive for a long time with a larger and larger proportion of their members driving farther and farther. But eventually—as we can see from the experience of the Metropolitan Regional Churches built a half-century ago—they also will be affected. By the time competition from large suburban churches and awareness of community "problems" forces them to rethink their situation, the community may be almost solidly black for many miles.

It may be thought that a Special Purpose Church would be in the best position to survive, even in the post-transitional community. Its highly selective membership often travels great distances. Few, if any, of the members may live nearby. It would seem that their members would travel anywhere to go to this type church. But this is not so, from our observation.

In the earlier stages of community transition, problems may be minimal for the Special Purpose Church. But later, a sense of alienation often emerges when the race of the congregation is different from that of the neighborhood. White people may feel uncomfortable going into the unusual situation where they are the minority. This alienation is usually expressed by the members of the congregation as fear for their safety while walking from their cars to the church.

After a while, as community transition progresses, even Special Purpose Churches usually move to "better" locations—which almost invariably are "whiter" areas.

For the most part, the church that has gone through a gradual process of transition has been a neighborhood church before, during, and after the community transition. Its emotional identification with the community made it sensitive to the changes as they began to occur. Its image of itself as a church that serves a particular community led it to reach out to the newcomers and to alter its program to meet their needs. Its previous status in the community and its role as a center of community activities made it attractive to the newcomers as they sought to put down roots in the new place. As the neighborhood changed, the church changed, too.

On the other hand, most churches that resisted gradual

transition either never were community churches, or had lost contact with their communities long before racial transition began to take place—they had become what Lyle E. Schaller calls ex-neighborhood churches.

> A decreasing proportion of the members lived within walking distance of the building and a rapidly decreasing proportion of the residents identified with what earlier often had been *the* neighborhood church. . . . What had once been two "communities" (church and neighborhood) with a very high degree of overlap between the two, became two separate communities with very few people members of both communities.[2]

2. Self-Image

Churches tend to have identities, long-term concepts of themselves, and images in the minds of the people of the community. They are "First Church" or "Hazel Park Church" or "Dr. Hinkle's church." They understand who they are and they know their traditions and strengths. Many churches have a second identification ("The Friendly Church in the Big City") or a motto ("Enter to Worship, Depart to Serve") or an identifying image, with a slogan ("The Church of the Lighted Tower") that captures and preserves that image.

Such a self-concept is necessary and desirable for a congregation. If the church is in a stable environment, this guiding self-concept may remain potent for many years, but it becomes a problem if it is no longer appropriate or realistic. How can it continue to be "Dr. Hinkle's Church" when he is dead or gone? How can it be "The Church of the Lighted Tower" when the congregation can no longer afford to keep the lights burning? How can it continue to be "Jefferson Heights Church" when the people of the congregation no longer live in Jefferson Heights community, but drive in from surrounding suburbs?

The self-concept of individuals is often closely identified

with their image of their church. Sociologists have noted that one of the functions of religious institutions is to provide "social location"—that is, to help the individual locate him- or herself in social space.

Changing a congregation's self-image may involve changing the self-image—or even the social location—of many of its members. They may resist change, for the very reason that the change involved is so fundamental to their personalities. This may help to explain the observation of many consultants who work with local churches that the people who are most loyal to the church are those who find it most difficult to change. Extreme loyalty comes from finding a great deal of personal meaning in the church, just the way it is, or the way it was. That meaningfulness becomes an impediment, when change is necessary.

We visited one church in a quiet neighborhood with tree-lined streets, into which middle-class black families had been moving. The church building was immaculate, and the grounds were neatly trimmed. As we drove up, an elderly white man was lovingly weeding the shrubbery. The white congregation had dwindled to a handful, most of them over seventy years of age. The finances were in terrible shape, but rather than accept subsidy for a full-time pastor (whom the judicatory insisted must be black), they had asked for a part-time seminary-student pastor. "Give us just two more years," they had said. "By then most of us will have had our funerals, and then you can do with the building whatever you like."

This rather pathetic story illustrates a common theological problem in churches in transitional communities. People often cannot separate the institutional church from themselves. Their reluctance to see the church change may be based on their inability to handle their own deaths. If it dies (changes), then they too die.

This insight has been warmly received during training

sessions with pastors of churches in transitional communities. It is one of the most important clues to the dynamics of congregational change.

To understand the mechanisms of change in the white church, perhaps it would be helpful to draw an analogy from the response of individuals to personal crises. "When confronted with a crisis, an individual goes through four phases as he/she comes to grips with the reality of the problem and responds: (1) shock, (2) defensive retreat, (3) acknowledgment, (4) adaptation and change."[3]

Shock occurs when the person perceives the reality of the crisis and feels the impact of the implications. Avoidance seems to be built into most living organisms—one of the first reactions to a crisis is withdrawal. The withdrawal is usually a retreat into a defensive posture of denial (It can't be true), or a determination to resist change (I won't let it happen), or apathetically going through routinized, familiar motions (washing the dishes while crying over the loss of a loved one).

Just as an individual reacts to a crisis with disbelief or bewilderment, so does a congregation—particularly, its leadership. They may seem paralyzed, or they may flounder about in uncertainty.

The second stage of reaction to a crisis is often retreat into the traditional. A church may try to avoid change by doing the "old" things bigger and better. Programs that once "packed the place" may be dusted off and updated slightly. Long-range planning often gets shorter and shorter in time frame, until a conspiracy of silence settles over the church and planning for the future becomes a forbidden topic. No one mentions in public meetings the crisis they all know is present and pressing.

The ultimate in retreat for the individual is withdrawal from the organization. Some persons are unwilling or unable to change their concept of the church, so they leave and go to another church. Some congregations are unwilling to change their self-concept in order to minister to the newcomers; for them, the final retreat is to relocate or to close, rather than to change.

Healthy individuals eventually recover from their shock and begin to rejoin life. In the third stage of adaptation, some of the leaders of the congregation acknowledge the situation, begin to confront those who are still reluctant, try to build coalitions of support with those who are about to leave, and begin to explore the realities of the new situation, searching for ways to respond.

Outside resource persons and research studies can be especially helpful at this stage by helping the congregation understand its situation and by bringing a neutral perspective to a problem-solving process that may be stalled for lack of information and tangled by interpersonal conflicts.

However, there is one important difference between an individual and an organization. An individual inevitably ages and eventually leaves the physical world. But an organization can become young again in this life—it can be renewed and revitalized!

Rejuvenating a congregation does not necessarily mean making a complete break with past traditions. As a matter of fact, the old-timers will find it easier to continue to participate during the transition, if the new directions are seen, in some way, as a continuation of the existing tradition. Jefferson Heights Church may be reclaimed as a neighborhood church, serving the people of the community—except that the people's color is different. Dr. Hinkle may be replaced by The Reverend Stevens, but the congregation may again rally around a strong pastoral leader.

However it originates, the new self-concept must be realistic in its assessment of the community situation, feasible in terms of available and potential resources, viable in the understanding of the leaders, and powerful enough in the hearts of the congregation to motivate them to move into the future, with its unknown challenges and opportunities.

3. Church Program

A white congregation in a transitional community, which is changing from white to minority, must find ways to overcome at least three barriers.

a. *The Age Gap.* The natural mobility of younger persons means that younger members of the congregation often scatter across the country. The attraction of family life in the suburbs means that young couples tend to move out of inner-city neighborhoods when children arrive—or that they never settle there in the first place. Older members are more stable: They remain in the neighborhood, or they return to attend the church out of loyalty.

So the church in a transitional community is usually a congregation of older members, who are trying to reach new people from a community where the average age is considerably less. This is a difficult task, aside from the added complication of difference in race.

b. *The In-Group/Out-Group Gap.* Social psychological analysis of groups points out that every group has a we/they quality. There are always those who belong and those who do not. Positive feelings for in-group members are usually matched by negative feelings toward nonmembers (members of the out-group). Notice that this is a common human trait and is not necessarily related to racial attitudes.

When studies are made of local churches, people often report that one of their congregation's major strengths is that they are "friendly people." They may become quite hostile to a consultant who points out to them that this is friendliness toward one another and that a stranger may not have the same experience.

Social psychologists also hypothesize that external conflict may serve to strengthen internal cohesiveness. Just as some politicians have tried to unify the country by frightening the populace with external enemies, some congregations may unite to resist external foes. Sometimes the external threat is the neighborhood; sometimes it is the judicatory. Uniting against either "foe" can be disastrous for a congregation in a transitional community. If they unite to resist the emerging community, they are trying to hold back the inexorable future, and this usually results in increasing their alienation from their only potential source of new members. If they unite to resist the mission strategy of the judicatory, they may be ignoring the best available counsel and help from within the church.

c. *Social Class.* Studies are inconclusive as to whether racial transition in communities is necessarily accompanied by a change in social class. Some observers assume that since there are more Blacks in the lower socio-economic level, it necessarily follows that community change involves a reduction in social class.

Studies of mobility, however, have shown that it is the more highly educated and affluent who move. This would mean that the black "pioneers" would be of a higher socio-economic level, perhaps even higher than the Whites remaining in the community. A lower-income white congregation may not be very attractive to a highly educated black newcomer to the community.

An integrated local church flies in the face of some of the most resistant attitudes in American society today. In such a church, people must not only cross racial lines to participate in the same organization, but they must intermingle socially, since this is characteristic of the informal structure of the congregation—and they must pay for the privilege of doing so.

White church leaders are very much aware of the difficulty of persuading white church members to accept Blacks. And leaders in churches in transitional communities have become painfully aware of the difficulty of persuading Blacks to enter predominantly white churches.

Lawrence Lucas was referring to the Roman Catholic Church, but his comments might apply to most predominantly white denominations as well.

> Black people are not leaving the Church. They are waking up to the reality that the Church has left them and is not making any steps toward them. So they have stopped running after the white church just as they have the white-everything-else.[4]

In adapting the church program to new people, the burden falls heavily on the pastor. Often the congregation contains no one—or only a handful of persons—from the group for which the new programs must be developed. The pastor must locate willing persons in the community, become their friend, nurture their relationship to the church, develop them as leaders, and in general, "carry" the new program through its fledgling stage. This may take several years of intentional effort and hard work.

Patterns of Transition in Churches

From place to place and from time to time, churches vary in how soon they begin to change and how rapidly they change, compared with the transition in the community.

Some churches have gone through a gradual transition. As the communities changed, so did the congregations. Typically, the percentage of Blacks in the congregation was somewhat less than in the community, but not much less. As the community changed, the church continued to change. Eventually the church has become a black congregation in a black community. It remains at the same location, belongs to the same denomination, and usually even retains the same name. This does not mean that major changes did not occur, but that these changes happened gradually, and that there was a sense of continuity.

By contrast, the second pattern is one of discontinuity. At some point in time, the white congregation dissolved and an all-black congregation inherited the building. Usually it was necessary for the black congregation to purchase the building, but in a few cases the white congregation *gave* the building to a black congregation, or only a nominal amount of money was involved. Sometimes there was a merger of a white church and a black church, or the denomination may have relocated a white congregation out of the building and put a black congregation into it. An extreme example of discontinuity occurs when the white congregation disbands, and the property is reused for a completely different form of ministry, such as a community center, or is sold for nonchurch use.

Figure A represents two general patterns of gradual transition, and one of discontinuity, in relation to the transition in the community.

<u>Figure A</u>. Patterns of Congregational Change

Over a period of time the community (1) changes from all-white to all-black. The transitional church (2) changes at roughly the same rate as the community. The integrated church (3) remains racially mixed, even though the community has changed. Patterns of discontinuity (4) involve an abrupt change in the racial composition of a congregation, through dramatic shift in program, change in the racial composition of the staff, merger, or sale of the building.

1. The Transitional Congregation

In many metropolitan areas across the country there is at least one congregation which once was a white congregation in a white neighborhood, but now is a black congregation in a black neighborhood. The historical pattern is simple—during the years of transition in the community, the church was in transition, too.

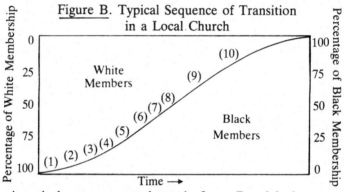

Figure B. Typical Sequence of Transition in a Local Church

A typical sequence, as shown in figure B, might be:

(1) A black youngster attends Sunday school.
(2) A black family joins the church.
(3) More black youngsters begin to attend the Sunday school.
(4) More black adults join the church.
(5) Blacks participate in organizations within the church—choir, Sunday school, women's society.
(6) A black person assumes a visible leadership role. This may be a symbolic position, rather than one of great influence and power.
(7) Several Blacks move into decision-making positions.

(8) There is a black majority in some activities, there have been major program changes to accomodate the needs and desires of the incoming group, and a significant number of Blacks are in positions of authority.

(9) A black pastor is appointed.

(10) Some Whites may remain for ten or more years. Those who stay usually hold major offices. Some Whites may join, but the congregation has become essentially a black congregation in a black community.

There are, of course, variations in this sequence. It sometimes happens that the first Blacks are adults who attend worship, rather than youngsters in Sunday school. Frequently, the white Sunday school has become practically defunct, or it has dwindled to merely one adult class of elderly persons.

A second variation is the way Blacks enter the leadership. The pattern depends upon the talents and interests of the incoming group. Sometimes they enter into leadership quickly and easily; sometimes they are reticent to take such roles.

A third variation concerns the pastor and/or staff. Some churches, lacking black leadership and/or wishing to change their image, have added a black assistant pastor or parish worker, or a black pastor was brought in early in the transition, when the congregation was still predominantly white.

The diagram of the typical sequence (figure B) was based on percentages, but obscures another typical pattern—an overall *decrease* in membership, amounting to 50 percent or more. Figure C is also stylized, but it is a more accurate portrayal of some of the typical patterns.

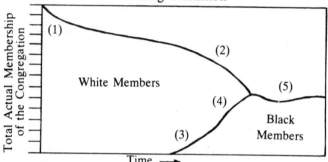

Figure C. Typical Sequence of Church Membership During Transition

(1) The actual membership of the white congregation usually has been declining for some time prior to racial transition in the community. Sometimes this loss had not been reflected in the *reported* membership figures, and the congregation is rudely awakened to its real strength when a new pastor comes in and cleans the rolls.

(2) Net membership loss often continues, even after Blacks begin to enter the church, because Whites leave faster than Blacks join. At this point, the internal strength of the congregation may be rising, although statistical indicators do not reflect it.

(3) The speed of the transition varies greatly. The longer a congregation holds out against the changing community, the faster the transition in the church is likely to be, once it starts, and the greater the overall decline will probably be.

(4) Some churches which became integrated in the late 1950s or early 1960s maintained some Whites in the congregations for ten to fifteen years. Some still have a few white members. And some Whites join predominantly black churches.

(5) The end result of the transition is essentially a new congregation of a different race. The total membership of the new black congregation is usually less than half that of the

previous white congregation, and it may or may not ever equal the numerical strength of the white congregation in its heyday.

2. *The Stalled Congregation*

The most common type of church in transitional communities is the "stalled" church. It is stalled, resisting change, and firmly gripped by organizational paralysis. The congregation is paralyzed by fear of the future, lacks a sense of direction, and is unable to respond to leadership initiatives.

Oddly enough, overt conflict is usually absent. This does not mean that there are no differences of opinion, but rather that there are no acceptable ways to deal with those differences. And the inability to handle those differences helps to stifle creativity in the congregation.

Leas and Kittlaus, in their book *Church Fights,* point out that conflict is desirable, since disagreements are out in the open, are recognized, and since there is energy within the church to search for a solution. Stalled churches are "non-conflict" situations. Their inventiveness and creativity are focused on efforts to avoid conflict, rather than on developing better ways to deal with disagreements or on searching for solutions. They identified three types of non-conflict situations typical of stalled churches: paralysis of fear, withdrawal, and lack of planning.

Fear of impending doom—that is, fear of a hypothetical situation, leads to despair about what *might* happen.

> Fear of impending doom is sometimes felt by just one person. Somehow, somewhere in a local church will emerge a graduate, experienced, credentialed *doomsayer*. His (or perhaps their) job will be to frighten everybody to petrification every time there is a possibility of acting. . . .
>
> The rest of the congregation goes around with internalized, intrapersonal conflict ("I wish I had the guts to stand up to that doomsayer"), and a feeling of dissatisfaction that they "aren't doing anything." When the congregation confronts the

doomsayers, there is a real possibility of conflict, but when the doomsayers are allowed to "win," we do not have conflict, only dissatisfaction.[5]

The second type of non-conflict is withdrawal. Obviously, there can be no conflict—or search for a solution—unless at least two sides are willing to do battle.

Occasionally—very occasionally—a group of white people walk out of a church *en masse,* rather than remain and fight about the future of the congregation. One white layman came to his pastor and said, "I thought I owed it to you to tell you that forty of us are going to get up in the middle of the service today and walk out." The pastor replied, "All right, but understand one thing. You are not walking out on me; you are walking out on God."

Pastors worry about this kind of mass withdrawal, but it rarely happens. A more typical pattern is for individuals to slip away without a word, or to take advantage of the slightest "legitimate" reason to transfer their memberships. Even those who threaten to quit the church often do not do so—unless they are forced to take a public stand and must leave in order to save face. Withdrawal is not a comfortable solution for people who have long-standing loyalty and strong ties to a congregation. The threat to withdraw may be the worst thing they can think of. But when they actually contemplate doing it, they often realize that it is they who would be the greater losers. At that point, they often decide to stay and make the best of the transition.

Many churches in racially changing communities evidence the final type of non-conflict situation identified by Leas and Kittlaus—lack of planning. Conflict can be avoided if there is no way for people to participate in the planning. They can't say what they are thinking since there is no forum for the dispute.

Why does a congregation permit this unsatisfactory condition? They are afraid and bewildered. They may fear that if the conflict ever surfaced, they would not be able to handle it. The attitude that "Christians don't argue" has prevented many congregations from gaining experience in successfully dealing with emotionally charged disagreements. In their already weakened condition, they may be afraid of losing members or strength needed for survival.

The stalled congregation may be floundering for lack of a clear sense of direction. If there are no other churches nearby which have successfully gone though transition, they may have no models to follow. They may feel that they are all alone, sailing uncharted seas, attempting the impossible. Many complain, "We've tried everything." Of course, they have not really tried *every*thing; actually, they've tried very little.

3. *Patterns of Discontinuity*

Patterns of *dis*continuity are ways of starting over. The church building remains, but the congregation that occupies it is essentially a new one, having little or no sense of continuity of mission with the former white congregation.

a. *Sale of the Building.* As one drives through an established black community and looks at the churches, one may become aware that most of the church buildings are not occupied by the original owners. Former synagogues may still have the Star of David window. Cruciform buildings obviously once belonged to formal liturgical denominations. "Akron-plan" buildings are relics of the heyday of the Sunday school movement in the so-called "mainline Protestant denominations."

A typical scenario involves a white congregation that tried to maintain itself as an all-white church while the community changed. They may have made no real effort to attract the newcomers; or they may have made half-hearted attempts, after the major change in the community was past. Recruiting no new members from the community, and few from anywhere, they dwindled in leadership and financial resources until the leaders finally gave up the struggle and sold the building to a black congregation. At that point, the white church may have merged with another white congregation and relocated; they may have used the proceeds of the sale to build themselves a new building; or they may have disbanded, the members transferring wherever they wished.

Sometimes the congregation doesn't linger long. One church still had 450 members on the rolls at the time they discontinued services.

The disposition of the assets of a church building that has been sold varies, by denomination and by region.

Most predominantly white congregations who wish to sell do not have black congregations of their own denomination in the same community to whom to sell (or give) property, so they sell on the open market. In most of these denominations, the proceeds of the sale belong to the congregations, to use as they see fit. The local congregation, being autonomous, can make its own decisions. Usually the money is reinvested in another church building at a location more suitable for ministering to the present (white) congregation.

On some occasions the real estate transaction leaves behind not only a sense of discontinuity, but a feeling of alienation and of having been "ripped off." The negotiations may have been sharp and heated. The black congregation, which was looking forward to the new building, sadly discovers that it has inherited a white elephant with high energy costs and deferred maintenance.

b. *Intentional Transfer of Property*. Usually a white congregation sells its property to the highest bidder. There have been occasions, however, when they have transferred the building to a black congregation with a sense of intentionality. One white church had a "special relationship" with a particular black church, having helped them out in various ways over the years. When the community changed, the white church helped them buy the building.

If a church building is strategically located and structurally appropriate to serve the emerging minority community, the denomination may try to find a way to utilize the property for a new ministry.

Intentional selling of property still involves closing a white church, perhaps after it failed to become racially inclusive. Property still changes hands, but by some method, the seller negotiates with the buyer about more than money. As one white denominational executive explained, "We felt that they (the black congregation) would carry on the kind of ministry we would have, but were unable to pull off."

c. *Merger/Relocation.* When a white congregation merges and/or relocates, it is usually a strategy of retreat. It moves to a new location, in a community of "greater opportunity"—that is, one with fewer Blacks.

As we have watched over the years, it is fascinating how often, when a white congregation relocates, it moves into an adjoining community, or an area into which Blacks move a few years later. It soon may be faced with the same situation again, and it isn't any easier the second time.

In a classic illustration, a congregation moved four times! It merged with another church and bought a site for a new building. But before it could build, that neighborhood began to change. It sold the second building, merged, and moved to a third location. In the course of less than three years, there had been two mergers and the sale of three churches, three parsonages, and two building sites. The congregation had accumulated, through the combination of building funds and proceeds of the various sales, almost a quarter of a million dollars and three electric organs! A revisit ten years later found a congregation of less than four hundred (down from a reported membership of eighteen hundred at the time of the mergers), located in a predominantly white community, but surrounded by predominantly black communities.

White administrators frequently look on relocation or merger as the answer to the problem of the white congregation in a transitional community. The church moves out of the area into a better neighborhood, and continues to be (or becomes again) a self-supporting congregation. This pattern should be seen for what it is—a way to conserve and move the assets of a white church.

In another city, a prestigious white church had been a symbol of resistance for a number of years. The neighborhood transition was complete, but they continued to hold out. Some attempts at using the building for community service gained clients, but few black members for the church. Finally, in a kind of "instant integration," they merged with a black congregation of another denomination, with both pastors remaining as co-pastors.

Across the country there appears to be an increase in the use of strategies of discontinuity, rather than strategies of continuity (transition or integration).

A report of *The Pacific Presbytery Self-Study* (May 1975) asked:

> Should we not, instead of attempting to save [white] congregations in the process of racial change, recognize that there comes a time when the best thing to do is to close the church or merge it with another church in a nearby area and to begin again in the area to organize a new [black] church?

That report makes three presuppositions: (1) White churches rarely go through the transition process and come out as healthy, growing black congregations; (2) white congregations rarely make the transition soon enough or without ill will and fear and so are unable to become viable black congregations; (3) new congregations established as black churches may flourish, because they are free from the built-in problems that result from transition.

In regard to suppositions (1) and (2), in almost every large metropolitan area, we found examples of black churches resulting from a completed transition process from white to black. Some still receive mission subsidy and could not really be described as "healthy and growing"—but they have survived. Others are self-supporting, growing, and providing significant leadership both in the community and in the denomination. Second, experience in starting new black congregations is fairly recent and is scattered. Results thus far are promising, but it is too early to be certain.

Nevertheless, the report is accurate in reflecting contemporary trends: Strategies of discontinuity are becoming more common.

The Church and Transition
in the Cities of the 1980s

The lessons from the past are clear: Residential segregation has been strong and pervasive, but many communities are now opening to minority persons. White congregations have had a dismal record of outreach to black newcomers during the period of transition—but there is some evidence that they are learning. But the cities of the 1980s are not the cities of the 50s or the 60s. New patterns bring new possibilities.

Racial transition once was fairly well limited to areas on the periphery of the expanding minority communities. But today transition occurs in other settings as well—suburban areas and even exurbia.

Not all newcomers to the cities are black. Hispanics, Asians, Pacific Islanders, and Native Americans have joined the long line of immigrants to American cities.

Recently a new phenomenon has attracted attention in the media: White people have moved back into some city neighborhoods, buying and fixing up older homes—a kind of reverse transition.

Each of these situations presents a somewhat different pattern of community transition, and hence a somewhat different opportunity for the church. New forms of congregations are emerging, and new congregations may be established following different patterns than were used formerly.

Transition in Suburbia

1. Community Patterns

The distinction between city and suburb is breaking down as some suburbs grow older and some parts of the city are restored.

In many ways, social trends are no respecters of political boundaries. Racial transition often continues in its accustomed path, regardless of city limits.

The black population in the suburbs has been growing almost as rapidly as in the central cities. Between 1960 and 1970 the white population in the suburbs grew by 27.5 percent, but the black suburban population grew almost as rapidly—27.2 percent.[1]

Since 1970 there has been a dramatic shift of patterns. For the first time since World War II the black population in the central cities of the North is not growing. There are two reasons. First of all, black migration from the South has all but halted, and more Blacks are returning to the South. Second, a growing number of Blacks are moving to the suburbs. Between 1970 and 1977 the number of Blacks living in suburbs grew by 34 percent. Blacks may make up only 6 percent of the population in suburbia, but one out of four Blacks who live in metropolitan areas now lives in the suburbs.[2]

Blacks are moving into four types of suburban areas:

a. The rings of older suburbs adjacent to large central cities are following patterns similar to neighboring areas inside the city limits. The black population often has continued in the same corridor, merely crossing political boundaries when necessary.

b. Older industrial suburbs (which are not necessarily adjacent to the central city) are also showing patterns similar to the older industrial central cities. They have racially changing neighborhoods, just as the cities have racially changing communities. In suburban Chicago, for example, the black population increased by eighty-five thousand in the twenty-year period from 1950 to 1970. Nearly two-thirds of this increase occurred in nine older industrial suburbs, such as Joliet, Waukegan, and Chicago Heights.[3]

c. Not all the suburban housing available to minorities is older. In some cases, new subdivisions have been built for Blacks. In other cases, Blacks and other racial and ethnic minorities are moving into new, integrated, suburban developments.

d. Much of the remainder of the black suburban population lives in isolated villages or unincorporated areas. Especially in the South, these semirural communities may have been in existence for a long time and only now are expanding or filling in.

In southern cities and cities in border states, as the white population has moved farther from the central city, it has moved closer to traditional, rural, black communities. Significant numbers of black families in the South and border states reside in what was the country. For a number of reasons these families never moved into town, nor did they leave the state. Now the city is moving out to them.

As the suburbs move farther from the cities, it is not at all uncommon to observe a housing subdivision being developed adjacent to what is ostensibly a black community. In some places, $70,000 homes are being constructed across the road from a black congregation.

In short, racial transition is not limited to inner-city communities. In the future, even more suburban areas can be expected to experience this type of population change, especially where there is a substantial black middle class.

2. Church Response

Many churches in older suburbs could find themselves facing the classic sequence of racial transition, as the black population spills over from the central city. On the other hand, these churches may have opportunities their city counterparts did not have. The rate of change is likely to be slower, offering more possibility for a community to remain racially mixed for a longer period of time. The cost of new housing in the distant suburbs may be so high that older neighborhoods will retain their desirability. Changes in attitudes among Whites and greater contacts with minorities may remove the element of fear that earlier drove Whites out of communities. White denominations now know that they will have to do a better job of reaching newcomers, and they will be more helpful to churches in transitional communities.

Suburban churches probably offer the best possibility for stable, integrated congregations that will continue to be integrated over the long term. They draw their members from a number of subdivisions and neighborhoods, so that the fate of the church is less tied to any one of them. The quality and range of programming will be attractive to many middle-class Blacks. Some of these suburban churches have been involved in community affairs and are looking for ways to live out their commitments. They could become vigorous integrated churches.

Rural black congregations are experiencing the movement of the white population from the city, beyond suburbia, into exurbia—the rural areas adjacent to metropolitan areas. While denominational planners are beginning to help rural white congregations adjust to the new populations, the black rural congregations should not be overlooked.

These rural congregations will obviously require denominational and judicatory assistance. In most instances the existing building will not be attractive to the emerging suburban community. New programs, outreach ministries, changes in worship format, and white staff may be required. Orientation of the black pastor and congregation, enabling them to see the new opportunity for ministry, may need to be provided through the resources of the denomination.

Ethnic-Language Transition

1. Community Patterns

To describe the nature of transitional communities from white Anglo to all the various ethnic minority groups would require a separate analysis for each group. The pattern of movement of Japanese, Korean, and Chinese Americans, for instance, has been considerably different from that of Native Americans. The settlement patterns and cultural and language variations make it impossible to outline a common experience for all. For instance, it is not accurate to assume that the nature of the Hispanic transition is the same all across the country. It would be necessary to examine the movement patterns of each group in its specific settings: Mexican-American in Houston or Dallas or Denver; Puerto Rican in New York and Philadelphia; and Cuban in Chicago, Miami, or Union City, New Jersey.

It must also be remembered that Hispanics and Asians are comprised of many distinct groups. Asians come from many nations, each with its own history, culture, and traditions. And although Hispanics share a common language, they also represent different nations and histories.

Hispanics, and occasionally Asians, sometimes become the predominant population group in a community. Miami, New York, Chicago, Los Angeles, Dallas, San Antonio, and other cities have some communities that are predominantly Puerto Rican or Mexican-American or Cuban or Dominican or Columbian. Estimates of the number of Hispanics in the United States vary widely, but there may be close to twenty million. Their rapid growth—and their concentration in certain urban areas—has increased their visibility and is pushing their population beyond traditionally prescribed "Spanish communities."

In the Southwest and in California, the Hispanic residential areas are not limited to the inner city. Several of the cities in this region were originally settled by the Spanish and center around a plaza. As the city developed, the Anglo central business district was established elsewhere, leaving the Mexican Section intact. In other instances, pocket communities of agricultural or railroad workers have been engulfed by suburban sprawl. These *barrios* became nodes for further growth and expansion.

Experience from other parts of the country indicates that in some larger metropolitan areas the Hispanic groups may form separate and distinct communities. In Los Angeles, for example, the concentration of Mexican Americans in East Los Angeles makes up 85 to 95 percent of the population in the census tracts—a concentration similar to the black population in Watts.

Almost half the Native Americans (46 percent) lived in urban areas at the time of the 1970 census, and that percentage has undoubtedly risen since then. Native Americans are somewhat more concentrated in certain areas of Chicago, Detroit, Minneapolis, Baltimore, and some other cities, but there is not a Native-American community in those cities, or even a clearly Native-American neighborhood. Native Americans do not seem to cluster together in the same blocks to form tight Indian communities with recognizable boundaries. A study of Navahos in Denver investigated their proximity and found that the average distance between them was greater than nine blocks. Even newcomers lived an average of three-and-a-half blocks apart (ranging from zero—living in the same apartment—to eighteen blocks).[4]

Certain communities in New York, Washington, D.C., Seattle, San Francisco, and some other west coast cities are heavily Asian. With the exception of the "Chinatowns," however, the concentrations of Asians are considerably lower than in typical black communities. In San Francisco and New York, property values reportedly have gone *up* near

Chinatown because of pressure to expand, in the face of recent migration from Taiwan.

When non-English-speaking newcomers come to this country, they often seek the security of their own people, the familiarity of their own institutions, and the freedom of expression possible when speaking their own language. For recent arrivals, friends and relatives are particularly helpful by providing temporary housing, funds, knowledge of the culture, information about jobs, orientation to the city, introductions, and so on.

In America all racial and ethnic minorities have experienced some form of discrimination. The degree and scope have varied, but some measure of exclusion and containment has been endured by all of them.

For some groups, cultural adaptation, economic assimilation, and residential desegregation seem to go hand in hand. However, in today's social climate of ethnic identity, many groups are ambivalent about the extent of assimilation they really want.

> "I don't believe we're going to fall into the melting pot," says Democrat Alfred Guiterrez, the State Majority Leader in Arizona. "All we're going to fight for is a piece of the pie, but in a pluralistic society. We want to keep our culture and our language so that we can survive culturally in the United States."[5]

The residential patterns of Asians, Native Americans, and Hispanics vary widely. While there may be relatively high concentrations of certain groups, which form distinct neighborhoods, other groups are more scattered throughout the general population. Some ethnic groups (and some members of ethnic groups) will have more choice of residence than others, based on income, skin color, facial characteristics, and the region or community in which they are located. If present population trends continue, the number of Asians, Hispanics, and Native Americans will continue to increase dramatically. It can be expected, then, that there will be higher concentrations of some of these groups in many communities. In addition, there will be a greater number of other groups scattered throughout many predominantly white communities.

2. *Church Response*

While a few non-English-speaking persons may be found in many Anglo congregations, newcomers to the city who do not speak English typically gravitate to congregations of their own ethnic group. Such language or ethnic churches are important support groups for people in a strange land. For many people, God somehow seems most real in one's first language, whatever that may be.

Many Protestant denominations had their historical origins as groups of congregations speaking a similar language. The Augustan Synod of Lutherans spoke Swedish, while the Missouri Synod spoke German. In the early years of this century many denominations provided missions for persons who did not speak English. In 1930, in Chicago, The Methodist Church had overlapping annual conferences for Germans, Swedish, Norwegians, and Danes—and in addition, the "English-speaking" conference included two Bohemian congregations and a congregation of Mexican-Americans.

Japanese-American, Chinese-American, Hispanic, and Native-American congregations have existed for many years as a part of the home mission work of the denominations. Even today, The United Methodist Church has judicatory organizations composed entirely of Spanish-speaking congregations and one consisting of Native-American congregations.

Today, it is not unusual for Anglo churches to establish church school classes or special ministries for newcomers who do not speak English, especially if large numbers of them arrive at about the same time—for example, Hungarian refugees, Cubans, Haitians, or Vietnamese. Sometimes these groups grow to the point of becoming a separate congregation, meeting at the same time in a separate room, such as a chapel, or worshiping in the same sanctuary, but at a different time (usually on Sunday afternoon).

A Southern Baptist manual on establishing ethnic congregations lists seven methods of "cross-cultural outreach."

(1) Sponsoring a . . . person or family . . . inviting them to meals and social events. . . . This type of ministry is especially effective among internationals, persons temporarily in the United States for study, training, or business.

(2) Bible study. . . . Scriptures can be obtained in almost every language spoken by persons in the U.S. The group may prefer to study in English.

(3) Home fellowship. This might include the singing of hymns, preaching, Bible study and social time. Many who will not come to church would come to the home of a neighbor or a friend. . . . The home fellowship should reflect the desires of the ethnic group, but they should be aware that the fellowship is sponsored by a Baptist Church.

(4) Literacy class. Many language-culture persons want to learn English. . . . In some cases, the language groups will want their native language taught to their children. . . .

(5) Class in Sunday School. The language class meets at the same time as other classes, but the lesson is taught in the language of the persons in attendance. . . .

(6) Department in the church. If the ethnic group is large enough, a department may be formed, with its own assembly period and graded classes. . . .

(7) Mission within the church. The group may grow to the extent that it will become, in effect, a mission meeting within the church building. . . . It is essential that the mission members have a voice in determining their own leaders and programs.[6]

Establishing new ethnic congregations is one way to affirm racial and ethnic diversity and pluralism. It is a way to make the evangelistic outreach of predominantly white denominations more relevant to emerging racial and ethnic communities. New ethnic-language congregations may be the only alternative to wholesale abandonment of these communities by the predominantly white denominations. The transitional community may well become a new frontier for the establishment of new congregations, and one of the major areas of membership growth.

In a midwestern state one denomination has set a goal of establishing ten new ethnic congregations. Two have already been established, and a third is in the planning stage. In that particular area this denomination has a long history of attempting to sustain transitional congregations located in racially changing communities. But after about twenty years of closed churches, small congregations heavily subsidized by the denomination, demoralized white clergy, and frustrated black pastors who have inherited small congregations in large buildings, they made a conscious decision to try another way to reach the newly emerging community. They will start *new* congregations, rather than continuing to try to maintain churches in existing properties. The leadership postulated that perhaps beginning anew, without a building, without the history of another congregation, the community would respond.

Several denominations are now examining the viability of this strategy. They are viewing the racially transitional community as a place in which new congregations can be started. While not abandoning the attempts of existing congregations to reach out to the new community, the creation of new ethnic-minority congregations seems to offer viable possibilities.

A shortage of ministers with the necessary language skills inhibits the establishing of new congregations for many ethnic-minority groups. Those ministers who possess the language skills often have difficulty in having their credentials recognized by judicatory or denominational committees. For several denominations, there has not been a shortage of Cuban or Korean ministers. A number of them have immigrated to America along with their fellow countrymen. Congregations have multiplied because they wanted to preach. They have started new congregations, hoping that when the congregations grow, they can become full-time pastors.

Transition in Reverse

1. Community Patterns

While all data indicate that the primary racial population change occurring throughout America is from white to nonwhite, that is not the only change taking place. In many urban centers across the nation, revitalization is occurring in the downtown areas or in portions of the central city. Much of the redevelopment is taking place on the edge of black community or even in the center of the black community.

Federal programs of urban renewal have sometimes cynically been referred to as "Negro removal." Former slums have been demolished to make way for new high-rise apartment complexes for middle- and upper-income persons, most of them white.

Somewhere in the mid-1970s there was a small but significant reversal in the decades-long pattern of white flight from the central cities. Initially, the number of persons involved was small, but the reversal was significant. The year 1974 signaled an increase in building-permit activity in the central cities. The federal Department of Housing and Urban Development (HUD) has demonstration projects on housing rehabilitation and code enforcement underway in forty cities. The Federal National Mortgage Association has pilot projects in eight cities, seeking to encourage private savings-and-loan institutions to invest in restoration and rehabilitation of existing homes. A 1976 survey of 260 central cities by the Urban Land Institute estimated that "some private rehabilitation is taking place in three-quarters of all cities with populations of 50,000 or more."[7] Recently, a bank in South Shore Chicago announced a major commitment to provide funding for commercial and residential rehabilitation in the South Shore community. This community, once upper middle class, has seen the virtual deterioration of its commercial strip and the dramatic decline of its formerly prestigious residential area. The news media commentary on the major capital investment to be made there coined the word "greenlining." Greenlining refers to the action of a lending or banking institution in selecting a given area which is facing severe decline and committing major capital for its rehabilitation.

In Hoboken, New Jersey, a total of 1,300 houses have been rehabilitated with private capital. In addition, 4,294 housing units have been rehabilitated, using a combination of federal programs, bank mortgages, local grants, and city-bank municipal mortgages. Hoboken is engaged in a five-year program, at the end of which the city will have redone 6,274 units, or about 40 percent of its housing stock.[8]

Variously called urban homesteaders, inner-city pioneers, frontier persons, municipal carpetbaggers, and saviors of the city, the people moving in are:

—Overwhelmingly middle-class and white;
—For the most part, well-to-do. A high percentage have two
   wage earners in the household and a total income of more
   than $20,000;
—Highly educated. A study of an area in St. Paul indicated
   that 80 percent of the heads of households had at least a
   college degree;
—Young. Most are in the 20-35 age group;
—Managerial or professional persons;

—Singles and childless couples, to a large degree. Many families are two-person households. Only a small percentage have more than two children;

—Affluent enough to handle the financial manipulation required in rehabilitation;

—Highly motivated, and concerned about improving the neighborhood;

—Rehabilitators are likely to be involved in social and political activities.[9]

In most cases, market forces and political pressures will favor such persons, to the detriment of the present occupants, who tend to be the elderly, lower-income families, renters (and therefore vulnerable)—and they also tend to be black. While city officials may hail urban revitalization as a sign that the city has "turned around," others may ask, Are these rehabilitation programs to be just another form of "Negro removal"—this time by private capital?

Federal home rehabilitation loans (available at 3 percent interest for twenty years) make former slums a good investment, driving the prices of homes out of the range of low-income people. In Washington, D.C., for example, $20,000 row houses, just off the riot corridor, are being restored and sold for prices as high as $80,000. Critics have charged that it is the affluent who have benefited from loan programs which were intended for the poor. Senator William Proxmire said, "Some of the people getting the loans have incomes of $50,000. I know of one husband and wife [in Washington] who each make over $30,000 a year."[10]

On the other side of the controversy, one recent HUD report noted that about 70 percent of the loans nationally went to borrowers whose annual incomes were below $20,000. "You also have to remember," said a HUD official, "that the lawyer who is making $40,000, who fixes up his property, also is paying property and income taxes and reducing the tax burden of the persons complaining about it."[11]

This back-to-the-city movement has been hailed as "the best thing that has happened to American cities since ditches were turned into sewers."[12] It has also been condemned as "a conspiracy" to reverse the political and economic power of Blacks in large cities. Some have called it "gentrification"—the return of the gentry, the affluent landowners. Others have objected to that term as rhetoric, reflecting an anti-middle-class bias, and used the term "displacement." If you are the one being displaced, the terminology doesn't matter much. One study by HUD concluded that the displacement is minimal. "Everything leads us to believe this is not a major national phenomenon with huge proportions of poverty people involved."[13] Other studies come to different conclusions. The Rental Accommodations Office of the District of Columbia is reported to have concluded that in Washington, D.C., one hundred thousand people—one-seventh of the entire population—will probably be displaced from their homes in the next four years.[14]

Since the displacement is a private act, no government relocation money has been available for the victims.

It would be easy to overestimate the impact of this urban revitalization. Reinvestment in the central cities is often but a drop in the bucket. It does not deal with the vast acres of unused land cleared by urban renewal and presently lying vacant in many cities, gathering weeds and rubbish. While 10 percent of St. Louis is greenlined for federally guaranteed loans by private savings and loan companies, ACORN, an association of neighborhood groups, has concluded that "90 percent of the city is being *redlined* and city lending institutions have invested only 5.5 percent of their total home mortgage money in the city."[15]

The rate of abandonment, especially of slum apartment buildings with more than three stories, continues unabated in some sections of the central cities. Rehabilitation is attractive in only a limited number of neighborhoods—usually those with large numbers of former mansions, nice trees, parks, and quiet streets.

2. Church Response

Some white churches held out against the neighborhood and successfully resisted receiving black members for so long, that now the neighborhood is changing back again. However, these churches are finding that the new, white, upper-middle income persons are not necessarily attracted to a congregation of older persons whose goal is survival, and they are learning that a congregation that has successfully held out against some newcomers doesn't necessarily welcome any newcomers— even those of their own color.

Other white churches are taking on new life along with the rest of the revitalized white community. They have identified with the restoration movement and are refurbishing their buildings, and (in a change of policy) now reach out to the newcomers. Several have obtained new pastors—younger and more aggressive than their predecessors—and moved the parsonage back into the neighborhood it left years ago. In the future, these churches will have two tasks. On the one hand, they will need to become even more involved in planning for the future of the area; on the other, they may need to develop programs for the remaining white senior citizens, who experience isolation as more young adults move in, and who well may be forced out by rising prices. Churches can help the government develop a more humane relocation program for those who must be displaced.

The movement of increasing numbers of Whites into the central cities will present a new challenge to existing black congregations. As the cities changed racially from white to black, new black congregations replaced the former white ones. For the most part, as described elsewhere, white congregations either sold their properties to black congregations or went through transition as they unsuccessfully attempted to create integrated congregations. The new black communities now include black congregations.

As the process of gentrification accelerates and more black communities become integrated communities again, black congregations will be faced with some of the same questions that white congregations faced a decade ago. As new white residents become a part of the community, will black congregations intentionally reach out to welcome and minister to these new residents? What, if any, assistance or prodding will be given by the denomination or judicatory? What program changes or worship style will need to be considered in an effort to reach the new residents? Will financial assistance be required in developing new outreach ministries to those in new apartment developments?

While it was clear a decade or so ago that white congregations should reach out to the emerging black communities, the challenge presented to black congregations today is a new one. Black and ethnic church leaders will want to explore this new area of mission very earnestly.

It has been said that, for too long, integration has been a one-way street—the movement of Blacks to white institutions and white churches. Now the churches may be given the opportunity to provide a more comprehensive definition of the integrated church.

Future Patterns for Churches

The complexity and diversity of situations have produced a variety of responses, any of which may or may not be appropriate for other denominations at a particular moment. From our interviews, we have identified six models.

1. The Task Force
When a denomination has discovered that a mission and ministry is needed in a particular emerging minority

community, one possible response is to create a task force composed exclusively, or primarily, of clergy and laity of that minority group. These persons, who represent the denominational concern, will have the responsibility for developing the plan for what is expected to result in a new congregation. Such a task force will usually engage a researcher, or will do its own research, to collect appropriate demographic data. Questions such as the following are raised.

a. Where is the black population moving? What is the social and economic makeup of the emerging black community? What existing congregations are present in the emerging community?

b. Where is a strategic location for a new congregation in the emerging black community? What are the criteria and factors to be considered in determining a strategic location?

c. What financial obligations are going to be necessary in order to undergird the new congregation? How long a commitment should the denomination anticipate? At what point should the new congregation be expected to assume some financial responsibility? What might be projected as the time when the new congregation should be self-supporting?

d. Personnel questions are most crucial, as is the case in the creation of any new congregation. Is an experienced pastor required? Can a recent seminary graduate be expected to provide the necessary leadership? What particular personality traits are necessary? What style ministry is anticipated, and what type person does this style require?

2. The Predominantly White Task Force with a Minority Consultant

In many instances, a denomination may sense a need to create a new congregation or ministry in an emerging minority community, but will have no appropriate minority leadership within its judicatory. In this instance, a select group of church leaders is named, and such a group may be exclusively white. These usually are persons sensitive to minority concerns, and they may have some experience in interracial or minority-group programs and projects.

The task force also may call on consultants from national staff, or minority clergy or laity of the same denomination, but residing in a different city or section of the state. Sometimes a social analyst or urban planner is engaged.

The crucial element here is that the task force have strong minority input and perspective as it does its work.

3. The "Probe"—Judicatory Decision and Assignment of a Pastor

There are occasions when a denomination senses the need for a congregation in an emerging or already-established minority community and calls or appoints a pastor to investigate such a possibility. The pastor called to the situation will assume the responsibility for gathering data from the community and for making a recommendation concerning the feasibility of a congregation, as well as its location. The denomination may expect that such a congregation will in fact be established. However, the decision will be determined by the work of the pastor. This model may not involve a committee or task force, but a judicatory executive will be the primary link with the clergy person assigned.

Some people may misinterpret these strategies as a way of maintaining segregated congregations. The issue is not segregation versus integration, but rather, What is the most effective way for congregations to minister to newly emerging communities?

4. Pluralistic Congregations

In Los Angeles, Miami, Chicago, New York, and some other cities, we found churches with three or more different congregations, each using a distinctive language and cultural idiom. Sometimes these included Blacks, Whites (Anglos),

and Hispanics, or a Black, an Anglo, and an Asian congregation, all sharing the same building; more often they
involved an Anglo congregation and several other language
groups.

The organizational arrangements may vary from a business
relationship of tenant/landlord to that of a single legal entity,
with one membership roll and a team ministry, but with
worship services in several languages. In most of the cases we
know about, the Anglo congregation owns the building, but
they were not always the largest or most vital of the
congregations.

Relationships between the congregations may be virtually
nonexistant. One Anglo member complained that he had
been a member of his church for over a year before he
discovered that there was a Hungarian congregation meeting
in the chapel on Sunday afternoons. Other churches really
work at being international congregations—"a miniature
United Nations," one described itself.

The congregations worship separately in their native
tongues, most of the time, although they do do some things
together—joint celebrations, Communion services, festivals,
and service projects—emphasizing unity within diversity. One
such church sponsored the resettlement of several Vietnamese refugee families, under the leadership of the Korean
congregation. Often there is one Sunday school, taught in
English by persons from several of the congregations. In
pluralistic churches, music is often used as a powerful force to
bind the people together—a way to communicate the "flavor"
of another culture, as well as a simple means to teach some
words of the various languages.

Having more than two groups in the congregation gives it a
somewhat different dynamic from a black/white congregation. There is less worry about transition, and more
commitment to universalistic values and emphasis on
maintaining a multiracial congregation. Many white people

seem to find it easier to affirm the ethnic experience of Asians and Hispanics than to accept the worth and authenticity of the black experience.

Having several congregations of differing cultural backgrounds sharing a building is not without its difficulties.

> Most of it [one pastor thinks] stems from suspicion based upon ignorance of other cultures. One group may consider another more aloof or more cooperative than the others. And some older white members still find it hard to accept the cultural mixture "in their church." And trying to organize four Sunday worship services, Sunday School classes, prayer meetings in . . . limited physical facilities also generates suspicion among some that their inconvenient meeting times may stem from discrimination. And those groups complain that their early or late hours keep down their attendance.[16]

The pluralistic church with its multiple congregations may not be possible everywhere, because there are not sufficient numbers of diverse ethnic groups, but where it is possible, it represents a significant type of congregation. It has a unique attraction. One mother drove in from the suburbs to bring her children to the church. "We wanted an international experience for our children," she explained.

The pluralistic church represents an attempt to tackle the difficult issue of affirming the individual differences that make people unique, at the same time providing a unifying organizational framework to bridge those differences.

5. Dual Alignment

Some denominations that are associations of congregations may encourage black congregations to become "dually aligned," belonging to both their denomination and a black denomination. This has been one of the major reasons for the success of the Southern Baptist Convention among Blacks.

It has also been done by the United Church of Christ. The

million-dollar stone edifice which once housed the First Congregational Church of Chicago is now occupied by a dually aligned "First Baptist Congregational Church."

6. The Integrated Congregation

The concept of integration has gone through several phases of meaning and acceptance. At one time it was meant to denote the presence of black people, or people of other racial or ethnic-minority groups, in white institutions. During the days of rigid legal segregation of public accommodations, an integrated institution was one into which a person of color could be admitted. At that time, integration was seen as the opposite of segregation (imposed and legal separation).

It was during the 60s that the concept of integration came under attack by some of its former proponents. As many Blacks and Whites viewed the character of integration, it became clear that the concept did not include the reshaping of the integrated institution, but merely the admission of black people. The concept was further challenged because it was white-focused. Integration meant that black people participated in white institutions, shaped by white values, and usually directed by white leaders. Integration did not mean a sharing of values, style, leadership, or power.

Integration should mean a recognition and affirmation of a racially and culturally pluralistic society—a society in which cultures, languages, and races interrelate so as to bring strength, depth, and diversity to the whole. Integration should not mean, or require, the giving up of one's accent, songs, or life-style, but it can be the framework in which diversity is shared and appreciated by all.

The Christian church must recognize that God speaks to and through people in a variety of ways. There are times when ethnicity is transcended, and the embracing of another's culture, style, or language is done joyously, without denying

one's own. One denominational executive has expressed it
this way.

> By integration, I do not mean a Black church with a few whites
> in it, or a white church with a few blacks in it. By integration I
> mean a degree of racial balance in which each member is able
> to name himself. It is Black Christians singing German
> chorales and Germans singing Gospel music. Integration is a
> rearrangement of power in which no one has domination over
> another.[17]

For predominantly white denominations, the question of
integration actually must be viewed from two aspects:
denominationally and congregationally.

At the denominational level, there are approximately
three-quarters of a million black members in six predominantly white denominations.

> Their distribution, according to numerical strength in these
> several denominations, is as follows: (1) United Methodist
> (approximately 400,000); (2) American Baptist (approxi-
> mately 200,000); (3) Protestant Episcopal (approximately
> 75,000); (4) United Presbyterian (approximately 75,000); (5)
> United Church of Christ, U.S. (approximately 3,000).[18]

In addition, the Southern Baptist Convention has about
150,000 black members. (There are no figures for the number
of whites in predominantly black denominations.)

For these denominations, integration is a fact, at least in
terms of black presence in the denominations. And increasingly, in spite of their small numbers in comparison to the
white membership, they are making an impact. Blacks hold
significant leadership positions in many of these denominations—not only at administrative levels, but at policy levels as
well.

At the congregational level, it should be noted that not all
churches go through the full course of transition from

all-white to all-black. Some congregations have been racially mixed for so long that they can legitimately be called "integrated." These can be distinguished from transitional churches by three characteristics: (1) They have been stable and racially mixed for more than a decade; (2) Blacks make up a significant percentage of the congregation, but the percentage of each race remains relatively stable; (3) new white members want to join.

Integrated churches are found primarily in four settings.

a. Some communities remain racially mixed, but stable. Most frequently such communities are found near a university or medical center. The presence of these institutions guarantees a continuing demand for housing for Whites, and often they can generate large sums of money and political influence to manipulate the real estate market toward maintaining a stable racial balance in the area. Sometimes, but less often, such integrated communities occur near the central business district of a large city, where new housing or redevelopment areas are racially mixed.

Churches that serve such communities can remain racially mixed as long as the community does.

b. A few large, prestigious white churches have attracted black members, usually in small numbers. The values of the congregation impelled them to accept, or reach out to, Blacks. Usually the immediate neighborhood of the church is white or integrated. The size and prestige of the congregation not only prevented a wholesale exodus of Whites, but continues to be attractive to them. In fact, the integrated congregation may be a positive factor in the minds of new members of both races.

c. There are a few churches that have retained a white majority and are "integrated," even though the community has a black majority. These are examples of the Special Purpose types of church.

In one interview, a pastor insisted that his congregation was neither transitional nor white. The majority of the members were white, but church program included a great many service activities for the surrounding black neighborhood. They were involved in many of the struggles of the black community, but the pastor and the worship style were "white," though certainly nontraditional. We tried to explain the nature of the community transition and transition in congregations. The leadership insisted that these patterns did not apply to them. Finally we exclaimed, "You're trying to be something no one else is. You're not a black church or a white church—you're trying to be 'green.'" "That's it!" they said. "We like that concept. That's exactly what we're trying to do!"

d. In some small towns where there is a small minority population—not large enough to support a separate congregation—the local churches include a variety of races. This is likely to be found especially in the rural midwest. If migration from the city swells the number of minority persons, and these small towns become more desirable, it is reasonable to anticipate that black and ethnic-minority persons will follow this trend, and small communities that already have some ethnic-minority population may be even more favored as possible new locations.

As more Blacks move back South, many are choosing the small-town environment, with its slow pace.

Whether or not the integrated congregation is a viable option today—or in the future—depends, in part, on the continuation of stable, racially mixed communities. If integrated churches were not possible in the past because their communities were in transition, then integrated congregations ought to be more possible in the future if communities remain multiracial. Some congregations may be integrated for fifteen or twenty years, or even longer. Some may be "integrated" for only a short while, and may, in fact, turn out to be transitional.

The future is always unknown and, to some extent, open to new possibilities. Robert K. Merton noted at least two ways to break the cycle of self-fulfilling prophecy: (1) "Only when the original assumption is questioned and a new definition of the situation introduced, does the consequent flow of events give the lie to the assumption. Only then does the belief no longer father the reality"; and (2) "Appropriate institutional change [may break] through the tragic circle of self-fulfilling prophecy . . . since the self-fulfilling prophecy whereby fears are translated into realities operates only in the absence of deliberate institutional control."[19]

In the future it may not be so rare for Whites and Blacks to live in the same communities. The rising economic level of many Blacks has greatly increased the housing options open to them. If the possession of economic resources gives people more alternatives, many Blacks now have them. In spite of negative comparisons on many economic indicators (unemployment rates that are higher for Blacks than for Whites, studies that show Blacks receiving less income than Whites for comparable educational levels, etc.), many Blacks have sufficient economic resources to live almost anywhere Whites can. These economic resources, and the possibility of legal suits to implement equal opportunity to use those resources, have greatly increased the options open to educated or steadily employed Blacks. Past economic limitations, which severely reduced their housing opportunities, are falling. In the future, free and open choice will be increasingly possible for many Blacks.

Many of the black families now moving into the white suburbs are on their second or third move in the metropolitan area. They are not being driven from one section of the ghetto to another by urban renewal or intolerable community conditions. They are experienced, sophisticated buyers. They know something about patterns of racial transition and will try to avoid situations they feel are undesirable. They have time and resources on their side.

Increasing numbers of white people are looking for stable

integrated or multiracial communities in which to live. For these persons, there is value in cross-cultural and interracial sharing. Some have already lived in integrated communities or have had positive interracial experiences in college, in the military, or at work.

In short, it is increasingly possible—and probable—that in the future, more communities can be racially mixed *and* stable. Not every community that is "integrated" will become transitional. As this becomes true, the possibilities also increase for stable, racially mixed congregations.

Strategies for Churches
in Transitional Communities

How can the church respond to the challenge of the transitional community? What should church leaders at all levels do to insure the continuation of congregations in these communities, or to adequately minister to the newly emerging community?

Strategies should be realistic, "pro-active," and innovative.

1. Realistic

A realistic strategy recognizes the communiy context and the congregational situation as they actually are, free from historic halos of former glories, avoidance, or excessive pessimism or optimism. We often asked white pastors whether they thought the major change in the congregation would take place during their pastorate, or under their successor. The vast majority answered that things could remain unchanged for a little while longer, but that the next pastor would be forced to deal with the situation. Their attitude seemed to be that they hoped to be able to get out in time to avoid the difficult task of leading a congregation into major change.

Some strategies are more appropriate and are easier to implement at earlier stages of transition; some, at later stages. In fact, from the point of view of a pastor or administrator, the period of late transition is one of narrowing options. The longer a white congregation waits before beginning to reach out to the new black community, the fewer alternatives are feasible. Earlier in the transition, strategies of continuity are possible. Later, such approaches are difficult, if not impossible to accomplish, and strategies of discontinuity become the only options available.

2. Pro-Active

To be pro-active is to act *before* something happens. By contrast, our observation is that churches in transitional communities are usually struggling to respond to changes that have already occurred. If past patterns are a reliable guide to the future—and there is every reason to believe that they are—then it is not too difficult to identify areas where racial transition is highly probable.

Once the potential transitional communities have been identified and mapped, the church locations and facilities can be evaluated. Churches at strategic locations should be given careful attention by judicatory officials and receive priority consideration for pastoral changes, if necessary, subsidy, and so on.

What about churches that are *not* at strategic locations? It is not necessary, or desirable, to provide resources for *every* congregation located in transitional communities. Some might be allowed to continue to exist as long as they can, under their own resources, but would not receive aid. The identification of strategic locations helps administrators to know where to focus energies and resources—and where *not* to. When a boiler goes out, or a request for an emergency grant to repair a roof is made, the question should be asked: Is this a strategic location for continuing ministry?

3. Innovative

Finally, strategies for dealing with community transition must be innovative. In a way, this may sound contradictory to our earlier statement that strategies must be realistic. To be innovative, however, is merely to refuse to accept the limitations of doing things the way they always have been done.

The story is told of a large truck that became thoroughly stuck under a low bridge. While the driver strained the motor, unsuccessfully trying to back out, and an engineer tried to figure out a way to jack up the bridge, a small boy asked, "Why don't you just let some air out of the tires?" Innovation does not have to be unrealistic; in fact, it may be the simplest, most realistic response to the actual constraints of the situation.

Strategies for Congregations

Strategies can be classified as strategies of "continuity" or strategies of "discontinuity." A strategy of continuity anticipates that after a period of time, the religious activities, programs, and services will continue to be provided by a congregation of the same denomination at the same location, probably with the same name. By contrast, a strategy of discontinuity intends that these will be provided by a different denomination, or that an entirely different type of service will be provided, probably by a different party.

As a matter of fact, both types of strategies assume a great deal of change. Neither type assumes that the former congregation can continue as it has. Both assume that sometime later, there will have emerged a new congregation (or a new mission unit), serving a different race, under new leadership.

White pastors and congregations often ask, "What can we do to attract Blacks from the community?" There are no easy answers to that question. The timing is as important as the approach. In the early days of transition, most churches occasionally had black visitors. From the warmth and sincerity of the welcome, Blacks could tell whether they wanted to return. They should have received at least as much attention as any other visitor: They should have been asked to sign the guest book or attendance registration, been introduced, received a follow-up letter or call. In one congregation in the South, the pastor had a reputation for visiting newcomers to the community. Whether they were black or white, he called on them within a few days of their visit. This served to reinforce and further personalize the welcome they had received at the church.

Many white churches have attempted to follow a policy of "We will permit them to worship, but we won't go out of our way to welcome them." The experience of dozens of churches indicates that this is a foolish, self-defeating policy. Because of their experiences of discrimination, a minimal welcome will not be convincing to most Blacks. But even more important, when Blacks visit a church, they are deciding whether or not that church is for them.

When attempting to involve new black members in a predominately white congregation, it is advisable to identify small groupings in the church where this can be facilitated in a more natural, easy manner. Sometimes a Bible study group, or adult fellowship group proves to be a good setting for new persons to become acquainted with other members of the congregation.

The pastor can facilitate personal contacts and friendships between black newcomers and white church members of similar age and family situation who would enjoy interracial contacts.

Special programs and drives may not always be necessary. Again and again, white congregations have become racially inclusive merely by continuing to do what they always have done. As the newcomers moved into the community, they were contacted and invited to attend. When they attended, they were greeted and welcomed. They received follow-up letters and calls and further invitations. The Blacks thus joined a predominantly white congregation on the same basis as anyone else.

In the early stages of transition, the strength of the program of the white congregation may be attractive to Blacks who are looking for opportunities to participate in church school, music program, youth groups, educational opportunities for youngsters, or fellowship activities for adults.

But it is important to remember that programs, however well structured, can never take the place of good, healthy, interpersonal relationships. The local church leaders, along with the pastor, should be alert to any dynamics that might impede the development of such good relationships.

We do not want to leave the impression that structured programs are unimportant. Our observation has been that churches can and have responded to the changing community through a variety of programs.

The nature of the program that will "work" depends on the community and on the needs and traditions of the newcomers. If pastors and congregations are sensitive, they can usually find usable programs. But they must look honestly at their communities. Some congregations had begun to develop a program which they thought was "black," only to discover that the type of black person moving into their particular community was not comfortable with it.

There are no "sure-fire" successful programs. Many types of programs have worked in different situations. Some churches have opened their building for use by community groups. Others have held special events of obvious significance to Blacks—for example, a concert by the choir of a black college. One church got started when a black serviceman was killed, and the family needed a local pastor to hold the funeral. Some churches have been active in open-occupancy efforts, helping black families find homes in the community.

The local congregation should participate in, or help to start, neighborhood organizations that are genuinely interested in maintaining the quality of life in the community, and keeping it a desirable place for *all* persons to live. Each organization must be evaluated on its own terms. Sometimes, active and visible participation in community-betterment organizations serves to identify the church as a group that cares about the community, plans to stay, and is concerned about the future of the area.

It is important that participation in neighborhood organizations involve others besides the pastor. Ministry in a racially changing community must always be seen holistically. The pastor will need to provide leadership both to the congregation and to the community.

B. Carlisle Driggers, reflecting on his own experience and his interviews with Southern Baptist pastors, concludes:

> It became evident that those pastors who had done the most effective job in leading their churches to begin an open ministry to the changing neighborhood had rendered a great deal of time to their senior members . . . [but] those pastors who had neglected the older members often encountered resentment and hostility throughout the church.[1]

Older persons, he points out, can be a source of support for change—if their pastoral care puts them solidly in the minister's corner.

> A pastor who does not recognize the value and worth of the older members to the total life of the membership is asking for trouble and wasting vitality. . . . The research indicated that as the older people came to know, love, and trust their pastor . . . and felt cared for themselves, they frequently had a compelling influence for good on the rest of the congregation as difficult decisions were being made.

> One pastor told me of a female church member who was confined to a nursing home. He or members of his staff would visit her on a regular basis. . . . When the church was

approaching a tense moment of voting to admit all races into membership, the lady used the nursing home phone to call her friends of long standing and urge them to vote in the affirmative, and not let the pastor and staff down.[2]

The longer a church waits before initiating programs designed to reach the newcomers, the harder it is to convince them. In the early stages of transition, it might be possible to include Blacks in the ongoing programs of the church without changing those programs appreciably. In the later stages of transition, however, when the community is more identifiably black, it is necessary to design programs specifically for them.

One of the most common efforts is a summer vacation Bible school recreation program. These have the advantage of being short-term, so that energies can be mobilized. They are specific and definite, so that careful planning can be done. Good resource materials are available, and it is a type program that usually is successful. And it is short, so that the commitment is limited.

Saturday recreational programs are a variation on this theme. These often are staffed by paid college students or operated by an outside group, such as the YMCA. This type program may have limited usefulness, in the long run. If the church merely hires someone to run the program *for* it and avoids getting involved itself, it is unlikely that the black community will experience a positive image. Most churches that tried this found that the program did not lead to worship attendance or membership of the parents, or even of the youngsters themselves.

In order to obtain adult members, programs for adults are needed. To help a white congregation get started with these programs, it may be helpful to ask a neighboring black church of the same denomination to send over some couples to talk with a group that is concerned about outreach. The black lay persons can share concerns, give some hints on how to proceed, and point out pitfalls to beware of.

One of the best possibilities is a couples group for persons of similar age. However, an older white congregation may have difficulty finding persons of similar age. This age barrier may be just as important as the racial barrier in reaching out to the newcomers; the rejection of the church by incoming Blacks may be based more on the age difference than on race. Nevertheless, where it is possible, a couples group is a relatively easy way to help new people make friends and become involved in the church, beyond just Sunday morning attendance. It is only as newcomers are made to feel that they are part of the social fabric of the congregation that they really "belong."

Really belonging also involves participating in organizations of the church, having friends within the congregation, making a financial contribution, and taking leadership roles. Active assimilation efforts will be needed in order to preserve gains that have been made and to move the newcomers into positions of responsibility, so that they can help to guide the church during the process of transition. These first black members and leaders are a tremendous resource for the church as it makes its way through the process of transition.

Property Considerations

Decisions about strategies, unfortunately, usually are dominated by property considerations. Most predominantly white denominations look at property in racially changing communities from the perspective of the past, not of the present or the future. All too often, they remember that St. John's has been "a great church," contributing outstanding leadership to the denomination, and that Bishop X was serving there when elected. This historic halo of bygone days may blind church leaders—both inside and outside the situation—to the present realities and future possibilities.

Sooner or later, the church in the transitional community must come to grips with the newly emerging black community. Some years ago, a minister, showing a national staff person around a community, said, "This community has no future." That is nonsense! Unless and until the millenium arrives, a neighborhood always has a future! That future may not be the one we want; it may not be a future we are prepared to enter; but the neighborhood does have a future.

Eventually, the physical facilities must be evaluated, not from the point of view of how they *once* were used, but from the perspective of how they *can* be used to serve a black neighborhood. Is the location a strategic one in the *new* community? How adaptable are the facilities? What facilities does the church have that will be needed in the new community? Are the operating costs (especially maintenance and energy costs) too great to be carried by a smaller congregation or by some outside subsidy group? Is the architectural style and design compatible with service to the new community?

Property decisions, such as the need to invest in the building (repair a roof, replace a boiler, etc.), often produce a serious discussion about the future of a church. Sometimes this leads to a decision to close, if the denomination refuses to provide the needed funds for deferred maintenance or a building emergency.

A good location for serving the former white community may not be a strategic one for the new black community. In evaluating a location, a number of factors must be considered: (1) size of area that can be served and the population of that area; (2) proximity to other churches of the same or other denominations; (3) relationship to sociological centers in the new community (stores, social service centers, places where people congregate); and (4) types of location.

There are two types of locations—regional and neighborhood. A regional location usually is at the intersection of two major thoroughfares and is accessible from an entire sector of the city. A neighborhood location is in the geographic center of a neighborhood or is adjacent to some sociological focal point, such as the elementary school or a neighborhood park. It may not be visible to traffic passing through the community, but it is obvious to local residents, particularly youngsters and people who are out walking. In the later stages of transition, most predominantly white denominations will have greater difficulty in sustaining a racially mixed congregation because the surrounding neighborhood is now all black. Such denominations can expect to reach a smaller proportion of the black community than of the former white community. For example, the United Methodist denomination reaches 5 to 10 percent of most white communities, but only 1 percent of most black communities. Other predominantly white denominations usually reach an even smaller proportion of the black community.

While a regional-type location is probably preferable, it is important that there be a residential neighborhood nearby. The church should not be completely surrounded by commercial establishments. In other words, a racially mixed or black church will need to be a combination neighborhood church and regional church.

In the early transitional stage, the church facilities can be one of the primary vehicles for outreach to the newcomers. The community may be lacking in facilities where new black groups can meet. Opening the church building to use by community groups can be a part of a deliberate strategy to identify with the needs of the newcomers, a way to get acquainted with emerging community leaders, and a chance to form coalitions with the groups and the leaders who will someday be the backbone of the community.

Decisions concerning the use of the facilities may be interpreted by the black community as representing the congregation's general attitude toward Blacks. If the building is used by youth from the community, how the trustees accept the inevitable wear and tear tells the community residents a great deal about their acceptance in that church.

The church needs to be sensitive to opportunity and flexible in the use of the building. One church was located across the street from a racially troubled high school. The students asked to use the building as a neutral meeting place, in an attempt to negotiate the dispute between the groups. Rather than seeing this as a unique opportunity to serve the community and as an *entree* into the emerging community, the trustees of the church were more concerned about the rule that there be no smoking in the church building.

In the later stage of transition, some capital investment may be required in order to adapt the facilities to new types of programs. Such an investment shows the new community that the church cares enough to change. Oftentimes the investment in physical facilities may be fairly modest, but it still may be beyond the capability of the congregation. Denominational help may be required.

In the post-transitional stage, property considerations are often completely dominant, especially if the white congregation has not begun to change. There may be only a handful of Whites left, and if the congregation has not begun to receive some Blacks, it is probably too late to begin. About all that is left is a building. Often, that building is overly large and has excessive operating costs, or it is suffering from deferred maintenance and would require a large investment.

The danger of vandalism makes it difficult to leave a building vacant, with the intention of reopening later under a new name and with a new program thrust. In the few cases where this has been done, it has been more by accident than by design. In some instances, the former congregations had collapsed and no one could decide what to do with the buildings. When the buildings were finally reopened, it was often found that the negative image persisted and that great effort was necessary to overcome it. It might be better for denominations to swap buildings, starting a new program in a different building, rather than trying to rejuvenate the image of an existing property.

Even if a congregation is successful in reaching out to the new community, it may eventually require capital investment to replace outmoded facilities or to provide adequate and modern space for new programs. Some sanctuaries will need to be replaced, or remodeled, for new uses. In one city, a former United Presbyterian building was remodeled to be used as a gymnasium for a United Methodist community center, which had been forced to relocate when a highway demolished its former building. In several cities there has been conversation about disbanding a congregation, tearing down the sanctuary, and using the rest of the building as a community center.

One strategy has been to relocate a black congregation in a building formerly occupied by a white church of that denomination. This may give the black congregation a new lease on life, a better building than they had before, and a new community in which to minister. If the black congregation does not have to buy the building, they can use their own building funds to rehabilitate and remodel their "new" building.

It should be noted, however, that many people in the black community are tired of hand-me-down church buildings. They know the problems of deferred maintenance and obsolete design of many of the buildings Blacks have inherited, and they want no part of them. At present, many black congregations can afford to build new facilities and are doing so.

Personnel Considerations

As a rule, a congregation does not outrun its pastor. We do not know of a single instance where a congregation began to accept black members when the pastor was opposed. A few congregations replaced a pastor and *then* initiated community ministries, but in general, a congregation does not lead its pastor. Of course, the pastor can achieve nothing alone; lay persons must be actively supportive. But the attitudes and skills of the minister are of crucial importance, particularly at times of greatest change. How this issue is handled varies from denomination to denomination.

Theoretically, those denominations in which pastors are *appointed* to congregations (rather than called) have maximum opportunity to utilize ministerial placement for missional purposes. In transitional communities, however, it rarely achieves that aim, because administrators usually have focused primarily on the needs of the clergy, rather than of the churches. The United Methodist appointive system, for example, has become overlaid by traditions of seniority and by other complicating factors, such as the size of the parsonage and the location of the spouse's employment. The appointive system is supposed to offer maximum flexibility in utilizing ministerial personnel, but its potential is largely unused in transitional communities.

In one city we encountered an interesting illustration of the use of the appointive power. An elderly white minister had the knack of maintaining a loyal core of elderly white people. He led them to resist the incoming younger black families. Finally, it became obvious that a change was essential, and the judicatory executive announced that a black pastor would be appointed the next year. The people resisted, but the executive remained firm—a black pastor was appointed, and a new black congregation was started in the building. Unfortunately, the story does not end there. The black pastor struggled valiantly, but it was too late—the church's image of resistance to the community persisted. Eight years later, the church was disbanded and the property sold. Meanwhile, the elderly white minister had a reputation as a good pastor to an older congregation, so he was appointed to another church, also in a transitional community, and he led yet another congregation in exactly the same pattern.

Other denominations with other forms of polity have different options and different problems. In the United Presbyterian Church, the presbytery notified a congregation in a transitional community that it would not approve a call to anyone except a black minister. The Ministerial Relations Committee helped the church find an able, mature, experienced, black minister, and the call was extended. When we visited this church, the black minister had been there just six months, but already some black families were beginning to join. The white members were staying and were responding enthusiastically to his leadership. They said that, regardless of race, their new pastor was more effective than the last several white ministers who had served that church.

The call system in some denominations has a disadvantage, in that the judicatory can intervene only when the pulpit becomes vacant, or when serious dissension develops in the congregation. The denomination may have few ways to encourage a necessary pastoral change. In some denominations informal mechanisms have been developed: Local lay leadership can be contacted and encouraged to press for a pastoral change, through the regular channels for that purpose within the congregation. On several occasions this has been an effective way to remove a resistant pastor and to bring in a new leader with different attitudes and skills.

When the white congregation requires subsidy, the national denomination and the regional judicatory have additional opportunities to intervene. Occasionally, in a number of denominations (Lutheran, Episcopalian, United Church of Christ) subsidy will be withheld unless the congregation agrees to change pastors and to call a minister who will lead in reaching out to the incoming black neighborhood. The power is there. But it is rarely used.

Sometimes, a black staff person is added to begin an outreach program in the community. In the early transition stage, this may be an effective strategy, if the white pastor is supportive of the effort, and the black staff person is skilled at reaching out to adults (not just to young people). A white church that waits until the post-transitional stage to add black staff often does so in the spirit of desperation—and it usually is perceived as such by the black community.

The best time to bring in aggressive pastoral leadership is *early* in the transitional process, when the community is only 5 to 10 percent black. It is essential that it be done before the community crosses the tipping point—that is, before the community becomes about 25 percent black. Beyond that point, it is often too late to follow strategies of continuity. The patterns of the community have become set—without that particular church.

When is the right time to bring in a black pastor? This is a question often asked. We do not know of any instance when a black pastor arrived *too soon*. There are dozens of illustrations of *too late*. All too often, by the time a black pastor arrives on the scene, the community has already gone through its major change, most of the patterns for the new community are set, the image of the church has been negatively established in the community, and most of the dynamic leadership and energy of the white congregation has dwindled. *Then* a black minister is told, "Now you take it and make something out of it."

In a large midwestern city, the United Presbyterian Church is experimenting in two situations, by bringing mature, experienced black pastors into predominantly white congregations in early transitional communities. In one of those situations, whites seem to be staying and responding to his leadership, in part because they simply feel that the black pastor is more effective than the previous white pastors.

The emerging consensus of many church leaders across the

country is that a black pastor should be brought in earlier in the transition process and left there long enough to become a stable element in the emerging community. Just as there is a "right time" to start a new church in a new suburban community, so there is a "right time" to identify with an emerging black community. Some white pastors can (and do) do that. It might be even more effective if a black pastor were on the scene to shepherd the development of the fledgling community and stayed to become a recognized leader in the later, developed community.

The issue of race and leadership is crucial. To be sure, a black minister in a congregation located in a racially transitional community will have considerable merit. However, the most important factor will be effective ministry, whatever the race of the pastor.

Financial Considerations

Finance is not a separate issue; it is related to the other considerations. Money usually becomes a problem when a congregation cannot maintain or operate its building, when it cannot afford a full-time pastor, or when it does not have sufficient funds to establish or carry on needed programs. Financial problems are but a symptom of problems in other areas: property management, staffing, program adjustments, membership recruitment, and so on.

It is typical for churches in the early stages of transition to be feeling no financial pinch at all. They may have an older, established congregation that contributes loyally and generously. Gradually that solid financial base may be eroded, as time and membership transfers reduce the congregation, and as fewer new members are received.

If a church resists the black newcomers as community transition proceeds, the church can expect to encounter financial difficulties—unless there happens to be an adequate endowment—as fewer and fewer members are available to support rising costs.

Even if a congregation does reach out to the newcomers, it still may encounter financial difficulties. The usual fear that there will be a mass flight of white members opposed to integration is often groundless. Rather than a sudden exodus, it is more usual for those who are not committed to the new directions to slip quietly away. Sometimes, this group includes as much as half the white membership—and perhaps as much as half the financial strength of the congregation.

During the transition, there is often a time when many of the white contributors have left, and there are not yet enough new black members to replace them. In addition, the new members may have had experience in black churches, which typically raise considerable sums through various events and special offerings. As transition proceeds, the church may have to change the way it raises money, as well as try to achieve a workable balance between income and expenses.

In the long run, it is not necessarily true that church income will be less. After transition, the black members will not necessarily have less income than the white members did. And besides, giving to the church is more a matter of commitment than of income. (Rich people do not always give more than poor people.)

Some congregations have been able to retrench financially and survive without financial assistance from the denomination. Sometimes they have been able to find outside groups to use the building, and the rental fees have been sufficient to pick up the slack.

Sometimes pastors who are particularly skillful in the art of "grantsmanship" can recruit funding from nonchurch sources, but this can become incredibly complicated.

There is a United Presbyterian minister funded by Title VII (Federal Government) funds for the senior citizens center and program. The assistant pastor gets 70 percent of his salary for his work with Project Reach Youth, a program run from the community center, and 30 percent to be educational coordinator for the church. The Hispanic full-time assistant pastor gets 20 percent of his salary from the parish and 80 percent from the Synod. The seminary intern who is full-time with the English-speaking congregation also gets 20 percent from the parish and 80 percent from national church funds. The community center coordinator is funded by the national as well for 25 hours per week.[3]

Some churches in middle-class black neighborhoods have been successful in attracting new members early enough and fast enough to replace the Whites who left. Not all churches in transitional communities require financial subsidy during the transition, but many do.

1. *Based upon our travels and interviews, some* observations *can be made regarding mission support to churches in transitional communities.*

a. There appeared to be no clear policy or criteria by which the churches were selected to receive mission support. In some cases, congregations were receiving financial aid solely on the basis of their expenses, with little consideration given as to whether the church was attempting to broaden its ministry or open its membership to the emerging community.

b. The amount of financial subsidy provided to churches did not appear to follow a predetermined policy. Local congregations of the same denomination, facing similar problems and challenges, and with essentially the same local financial resources, sometimes received substantially different levels of mission support. The differences could often be traced to the aggressiveness of a pastor or denominational leader, but sometimes the difference was the result of the past image of the church. Tensions among pastors and congregations may develop when there is this kind of inequity regarding mission support.

c. Financial subsidy, usually called something like mission support, often is given out with little regard to the mission of the congregation. Primarily, it means that a church is unable to fully finance its ministry, regardless of what that ministry may be. Such aid has taken on the connotation of ecclesiastical welfare, and some congregations have resisted receiving aid because they did not want to be made to feel inadequate, or the objects of charity.

In new suburban areas, financial subsidy has also been given, but there the congregations have usually felt they received aid because their challenge was greater than their resources. They understood that the aid was intended to be temporary and that eventually they must become not only self-supporting, but able to contribute to the denomination. Such expectations have not applied to churches in racially transitional communities. On the one hand, congregations and pastors should not be made to feel that they are objects *of* mission. On the other, "mission support" should be just that: support for a congregation that is *in* mission.

d. Few denominational judicatories have developed a policy or criteria regarding the length of time a church should receive mission support. In some instances, congregations have been receiving aid for more than fifteen years. When asked about the prospects of self-support or increased local financial resources, both pastors and lay people often seemed unclear or indicated that they had not thought seriously about the prospect.

e. For the foreseeable future, communities in racial transition will be part of the urban scene, in both central cities and suburbs. Denominations may be called upon to provide financial assistance for an increasing number of congregations. It becomes crucial that denominations and local judicatories have some clear picture of what their financial obligations might be in the future and what resources are available, so that they may plan ahead.

2. *Based on our experience, we suggest the following* principles *for mission support.*

a. Financial support should be future-oriented rather than based on the past. As funding decisions are being made, the question should be the *future* ministry of the congregation, rather than its past history. All too frequently, mission support has been provided because of the glorious history of a particular congregation. While this may be a valid criterion for a very limited number of historical shrines, for most congregations, the relevant question is not what it did in the past, but what it *intends* to do in ministering to the newly emerging community.

b. Financial support given to churches in transitional communities should usually be for a specific time period. Those churches must be held accountable to become strong, viable, self-supporting congregations, where possible. Of course, not all post-transitional black congregations can or should become self-supporting. But the lack of expectation, accountability, and intentionality has weakened their drive for self-determination and undermined growth possibilities. The issue of self-support can be a delicate one. All transitional communities are not alike—racial change occurs in poor, as well as in middle- and upper-income communities. Policies regarding financial support need to take into consideration the income level of the community, the potential income which could be generated by the new congregation, minimum operating costs (especially funds needed to maintain the physical facilities), size of the existing white congregation, and the potential outreach ministry to the community.

c. Financial subsidy should be provided for a purpose—a recognized, agreed-upon purpose, acceptable to both the contributing agency and the recipient. Annual goals for growth and mission should be set. It should be expected that as the congregation assumes more support, the denomination will provide less. For the health and self-esteem of the congregation, a timetable should be established (though always subject to review).

d. The amount of support should be not merely a token, but adequate to accomplish the needed tasks. One of the constant criticisms of public welfare programs is that the recipients receive just enough to remain on welfare. Too often, it seems that the denominations have been doing the same: The churches receive just enough to survive, but not enough to make much headway.

Many denominational leaders have failed to see that the church in the transitional community is, in reality, a *new* congregation. It has all the problems of a new suburban "start": establishing itself in the community, recruiting a congregation, finding leaders, developing traditions, evolving a style and an image. In addition, the church in the transitional community may have the liability of a large, antiquated building, which must be maintained whether there is a congregation or not. While the new suburban church may have the problem of lack of facilities, the church in the transitional community may be saddled with *too many* facilities.

When a new congregation is started in suburbia, the denomination normally makes a sizeable investment in land, parsonage, salary support, and program funds for two or three years, and a donation toward the first unit. As costs have risen, that investment now usually approaches a quarter of a million dollars.

In the past, no such amounts were available for churches in transitional communities or for new black or ethnic congregations. More recently, however, several new black congregations have been started on a similar basis to new white churches in suburbia, receiving adequate funding and support.

If these principles are followed, subsidy can have a developmental effect on congregations. Rather than pauperizing them or encouraging dependency, mission support can be just that—assistance to carry out their mission.

Equipping Pastors and Laity for Ministry in Transitional Communities

1. The Role of Theological Schools

No comprehensive strategy for ministry by the church is complete without identifying the role of the theological school. Theological schools are in many respects the life blood of the personnel system of the denominations.

As the schools shape their courses and curriculum, there should be more focus on ministry in racially changing communities as a specialized ministry. Courses and curriculum can broaden the students' awareness and sensitivity to other races and cultures and ethnic worship traditions; there can be courses on community organization and analysis, and even opportunity to develop language proficiency in other than Greek and Hebrew.

Courses on racism, intergroup tensions, and conflict management would be a source of help to those preparing for professional ministry.

The theological schools also can develop more programs in cooperation with denominational judicatories and local congregations, to help equip lay persons and local pastors already in racially transitional communities.

Some programs need to be developed for denominational executives and urban staff who have responsibility for comprehensive planning for various levels in the denomination.

Finally, the theological school has resources that can be utilized by the community in racial transition. They have students and professors able to assist in data-gathering and research analysis. Theological professors can work with congregations and pastors in local settings. Together, they can reflect, theologize, and strategize, for more effective mission.

2. Action Training

Theological schools are only part of the answer to the task of training persons involved in ministry in transitional communities. The laity who comprise the membership of churches in those communities represent a vast reservoir of talent and resources for accomplishing this ministry. Too often in our interviews, we encountered committed lay persons who bemoaned the fact that they lacked orientation to assist them as they endeavored to make their witness more relevant. Many clergy, too, will find themselves thrust into a ministry in the transitional community without previous experience or adequate training for this new task.

How can these persons be equipped?

We believe that regional and local-church training events offer promising opportunities for laity and clergy who find themselves in the midst of a transitional community. These training and orientation sessions have the advantage of being flexible in terms of duration and structure, content and format. The training sessions can be structured over a period of weeks, or even months, or they can be condensed to several hours, in a one-day event.

Many denominations are developing programs of action/ reflection training. These experiences are growing, and some experts maintain that this kind of training has significant and lasting input. As Paul Dietterich reported,

> Change occurs more rapidly in congregations when clergy and teams of key laypeople are trained together, jointly, in the local churches. Such conjoint and contextual training is far superior to the "cultural island" training event in which individuals, not teams, are trained, and where the training takes place far removed from the setting in which ministry must take place.[4]

3. Some Models

These programs have been used in various parts of the country to assist church leaders as they seek to provide a more effective witness and ministry in the midst of racial change.

a. Chicago Churches in Transitional Communities Program. The Community Renewal Society, a United Church of Christ agency, in consultation with local churches and other denominational agencies, developed a far-reaching comprehensive approach to the church in transition. The project was designed for some fifteen congregations located in the Chicago metropolitan area. The congregations were selected from pretransitional and transitional communities.

The program required a seven-year commitment on the part of the denominational judicatory and the local congregations. The denomination provides financial undergirding, as well as consultation. The congregations and the pastors agreed to a comprehensive program of training and consultation.

Unique in this program is a "covenant agreement" between the local church and the judicatory. The agreement includes: (1) local church (clergy and lay) participation in the "Training Program for Pretransitional Churches"; and (2) commitment of the denomination to develop, in consultation with trainees, the basic training design.[5]

The training design includes such areas as:

Goal-Setting and Program Planning.
The Theory of Church Organizational Behavior.
Evangelism and Renewal.
The Role and Function of Deacons and Trustees in the Church.
The History, Structure and Program of the United Church of Christ.
Stewardship and Fund Raising.
Christian Education Workshops.
Faith Exploration Workshops.
The Church and Urban Community Life.[6]

b. National Academy of Churches in Transitional Community. This training design was developed by the United Church of Christ, Vanderbilt Divinity School in Nashville, Tennessee, and the Association for Christian Training and Service (ACTS), a United Methodist agency. This was essentially a program involving analysis and diagnosis. The goal was to identify the factors affecting churches in transitional communities.

c. The National Workshop Model. Many denominations (United Methodist, United Presbyterian, United Church of Christ, Southern Baptist, etc.), the Joint Strategy and Action Committee, and others, have held national meetings. These have brought together denominational officials, pastors, and persons involved in congregations located in transitional communities, for inspiration, information, and the sharing of models for ministry.

d. Training of Consultants. Many church leaders have been assigned to work with local churches in transitional communities, but often, such persons have not had formal training in that task. Some denominations have created training events for this express purpose. The participants are provided with orientation to help them become skilled leaders in assisting churches in transition.

e. The Congregational Training Event. This training event is set in the congregation, with key lay leadership and the pastor and staff. These sessions range from all-day events to weekend experiences. In some instances they are designed to make the congregation *aware* of the nature and degree of change taking place. In others, the training event provides know-how and develops skills in those providing ministry in transitional communities.

f. Cluster Churches Training Events. This model brings together representatives of a group of churches involved in transition. These representatives may come from one denomination or it may be an ecumenical group. The purpose is to maximize training resources by exposing the broadest possible range of persons needing the resourcing. Often such events bring together ten or more churches. The design has included both weekend and one-day events.

g. Conflict Management Workshop. The trauma of racial change and the necessity to change, or to reevaluate existing values, often causes deep and constant conflict in congregations. The need for pastor and laity to manage that conflict skillfully has been apparent. Workshops have been designed to assist local church leaders in knowing how to identify, diagnose, and manage conflict.

h. New Approaches to Outreach and Evangelism. As communities change racially and persons of differing cultural and ethnic groups enter, most congregations that have desired to reach out to the new residents have discovered that their "old" approaches would not work. The methods successful with one cultural or ethnic group proved inappropriate for others. Workshops designed to provide orientation in evangelistic and outreach methods appropriate to these new emerging groups are essential for reaching many of them.

We have said elsewhere that in many respects, ministry in racially transitional communities is a specialized ministry. While it may utilize all the familiar skills of laity and pastors, most often it means acquiring new ones. The denomination and its judicatories and the schools of theology must not fail to adequately provide the congregational leadership with those tools essential to effective ministry in communities in transition.

Judicatory Considerations

The judicatory (diocese, conference, district, association, presbytery, or synod) may be a help or a hindrance to congregations struggling with racial transition. It is not often that judicatory officials or agencies directly thwart affirmative efforts by local churches; rather, they hinder by failing to provide the help they might give. These days, church leaders are rarely openly and overtly racist; rather, their long-suffering prejudice and ignorance shows up as apathy, lack of effort to learn, and selective inattention ("benign neglect").

In anthropology there is a term—ethnocentrism—meaning the assumption that the patterns and thoughts of one's culture are the right ones, and that others are wrong. This is often an unconscious process, and it does not necessarily involve ill will or hatred. Many a white denominational executive wants to do the right thing, but is prevented by the tendency to believe that he or she already knows what is best, without consulting black or ethnic colleagues, or the leadership in minority churches or communities. Failure to put forth the effort to listen and to learn is perhaps the greatest problem of white administrators in dealing with transitional communities. The needed effort requires more than spending time and attending meetings. It is a matter of attitude: a readiness to understand the validity of the black experience, and to acknowledge that it must be understood on its own terms; a willingness to be taught—an openness to new information and insights; and a flexibility—the acceptance of novel solutions as perhaps being appropriate in a given situation. White executives who are willing to take people on their own terms *can* learn. Many have done so.

Judicatories can play two important roles: support and intervention. The supportive role is appropriate when the initiative is being taken by the local people. If they apply for funding or request a personnel change or initiate a new program, the judicatory may respond. Intervention is initiative by the judicatory to stimulate change. The supportive role is appropriate as long as the pastor and/or the congregation has a clear sense of direction and is headed in a way that fits the situation.

Intervening in these churches is a tricky business. If a

judicatory official, consultant, or pastor "reads them the handwriting on the wall" too soon, it may trigger the self–fulfilling prophecy, cut off any opportunity for innovative response, foreclose any strategy of continuity, and hasten the demise of the congregations. On the other hand, if a congregation delays facing the realities of the situation, it may drift through the time of maximum change in the community, miss its opportunity for orderly transition, and "back into" a strategy of discontinuity (seal its own death).

The primary entry point for intervention by judicatory officials is pastoral leadership. A bigoted, inept, or frightened pastor *must* be replaced. Those pastors who are attempting to produce change must be supported, encouraged, and held accountable in their efforts to lead the change process. This does not mean that a pastor must "confront" the congregation in an antagonistic way. There are other, more effective strategies for change. It *does* mean that it is better for a pastor to err on the side of pushing too hard, than to risk missing an opportunity for change.

The normal and natural means for a judicatory to provide support, or to intervene, varies with the traditions and polity of the denomination. Some denominations are so strongly congregational that the administration has little or no way to undergird a congregation that needs help or to prod a church that resists change.

In The United Methodist Church, the relationships between the denomination and the local church primarily involve personnel, under the supervision of the district superintendent. The bishop (theoretically) can intervene at any time to effect a change in pastoral leadership. In practice, this rarely happens, however, because of traditional considerations of seniority and salary, and because of polity requirements that the pastor and the church must be "consulted."

Under the call system of providing pastors, the congregation virtually selects its own pastor, and the judicatory may have little formal influence. Informally, however, judicatory executives may channel applications, recommend particular applicants, discourage candidates, and in other ways influence the selection process. The greatest problem of this system is that of effecting a needed change. The denominations have few opportunities to intervene unless the pulpit is vacant.

Most denominations have numerous sources of funding: judicatory, national, designated gifts, partnership arrangements, and so on. It is difficult to maintain a consistent strategy, because the local people may play these sources against one another, receiving subsidy from one level to promote a strategy that others oppose. For example, the national level may believe that a particular church *must* open up to the emerging community, and they may deny subsidy until the church agrees to do so. Meanwhile, local funding sources may provide maintenance money, blunting the effect of the withholding of funds by the national group.

In one of the Lutheran denominations, there is virtually only one source of funding for mission outreach by local churches—the national church. This makes it much easier to coordinate policies and to maintain a consistent strategy.

Baptist groups are extremely congregational in polity, but they have a tradition of explicit printed resources (guidelines, manuals, how-to-do-it books) and strong executives at the judicatory level.

The "connectionalism" of the presbytery denotes a mutual accountability, which can be a powerful influence for change. Since decisions are made by democratic process, with a great deal of lay involvement, the presbytery may actually exert more authority than does a bishop.

Most denominations have various points at which local churches must obtain permission for certain actions. These opportunities permit the denomination to veto an undesirable option and perhaps to provide counsel in the aftermath of the confrontation, even though the judicatory may not be able to control the local congregation. For example, one of the early signs that a congregation is adopting a stance of withdrawal from the emerging community is the decision to move the parsonage out of the neighborhood. By refusing to permit this property transaction, the judicatory may help a congregation to confront its attitude toward the newcomers.

Denominations have developed various patterns for providing consultation to churches in transitional communities. Some of these are short-term, such as a weekend session; others are more elaborate and comprehensive. The first and perhaps most important phase of each of these is the contracting—the agreeing on expectations. This phase sets the stage for later joint activities.

The activities of consultants usually involve some combination of the following: envision potential, analyze the community, listen to community residents, clarify problems, set goals, and organize for action.

The development of a judicatory strategy for churches in transitional communities includes at least five steps: (1) Identify and map local churches according to the stages of transition in the community; (2) evaluate the strategic importance of each location for ministering in the newly emerging community; (3) determine the fixed cost of heat, utilities, and maintenance of each building and project the congregation's financial ability; (4) determine the present outreach program of each congregation, with special emphasis on the percentage of Blacks in the church as compared to those in the community; (5) develop policy recommendations and program to support congregations where needed and to intervene in congregations where necessary.

Conclusion

If we have discovered anything in the years we have been studying churches and communities, it is that racial transition is a complex phenomenon. The causes are multiple: racism, fear, the pull of suburban growth, the push of urban decline, crime, redlining, weak faith, and poor leadership. Viable strategies, too, are many: bicultural congregations, transitional churches, integrated congregations, expanded community programs, the establishment of new ethnic churches, and many others. No single strategy can be developed as *the* solution.

What we *are* sure of is this: The Protestant church and its predominantly white denominations need not abandon communities that are undergoing racial transition. They may need to change color or form of ministry, but they don't have to run. Multiple and comprehensive approaches to communities in racial transition will mean a continuity of ministry to communities as they change—racially, economically, or culturally.

Some strategies will require denominational intervention in matters of policy, program, and funding. Others will focus on leadership—leadership is crucial and should be addressed from both the clergy and the lay perspectives. Programs will need to be developed for theological schools, as well as special training seminars and consultation provided for congregations.

It is essential that denominational and ecumenical strategies be directed toward community stabilization and development, in concert with social, economic, and political institutions, if the goals of strong schools, good housing, viable community institutions, and safe neighborhoods are to be achieved.

Foremost for churches in racially transitional communities is a change of attitude. They have lived for too long in a fearful and desperate struggle for survival. Churches in racially transitional communities must live in a sense of hope in a God who is ever present. Faith and hope—not despair and pessimism—are the cornerstones of the Christian church.

The past does not completely determine the future. New patterns are emerging; new strategies must be discovered. In this book we have described the past; we have only glimpsed the future. Congregations, pastors, and denominational leaders with hope, imagination, and vision can write a new chapter for the church in racially changing communities. We think they can—we hope they will!

Notes

Introduction

1. Robert L. Wilson and James H. Davis, *The Church in the Racially Changing Community* (Nashville: Abingdon Press, 1966).
2. Editors of *Ebony, The White Problem in America* (Chicago: Johnson Publishing Co., 1968), pp. 7-8.
3. Gustavo Gutierrez, *A Theology of Liberation* (New York: Orbis Books, 1973), pp. 8-9.
4. Jurgen Moltmann, *The Theology of Hope* (New York: Harper & Row, 1967), p. 25.

Chapter 1. Dilemmas of Racial Transition

1. Quoted in John Hope Franklin, *Racial Equality in America* (Chicago: University of Chicago Press, 1976), p. 32.
2. Gunnar Myrdal, *An American Dilemma: The Negro Problem and Modern Democracy* (New York: Harper Torch Books, 1944), p. lxxi.
3. Ray C. Rist, "Race and Schooling: Key Policy Issues," *The Educational Forum,* May 1976, p. 514.
4. Gilbert H. Caldwell, "The Black Church in White Structures," *The Black Church,* vol. 1, no. 2 (1972), p. 13.
5. *Ibid.,* p. 14.
6. Edgar W. Mills, "Types of Role Conflict Among Clergymen," *Ministry Studies,* October & December 1968, pp. 13-15.
7. Donald P. Smith, *Clergy in the Crossfire: Coping with Role Conflicts in the Ministry* (Philadelphia: Westminster Press, 1973), p. 72.
8. Joseph H. Fichter, *Religion as an Occupation* (South Bend, Ind.: University of Notre Dame Press), 1966.
9. William B. Sapp, "Blacks in High Stress Jobs Should Quit," *Jet,* July 22, 1976, p. 5.

Chapter 2. Patterns of Transition

1. *A Report and Recommendations from the Task Force on Churches in Transitional Communities,* Virginia Annual Conference, United Methodist Church, December 1976.

2. Harold M. Rose, "The Development of an Urban Sub-System: The Case of the Negro Ghetto," in Robert T. Ernst and Lawrence Hugg, *Black America: Geographic Perspectives* (Garden City, N.Y.: Doubleday Anchor Books), p. 144.

3. Anthony Downs, *Opening Up the Suburbs: An Urban Strategy for America* (New Haven: Yale University Press), 1973, pp. 3-4.

4. Charles L. Leven, et al, *Neighborhood Change: Lessons in the Dynamics of Urban Decay* (New York: Praeger Publishers, 1977), pp. 132, 133, 127, 128.

5. Theodore McEachern, *How to Determine Transitional Communities in an Urban Area* (Nashville: Association for Christian Training and Service, n.d.) This is a manual for predicting White to Black or Anglo to Hispanic transition, using data from the U.S. census. The assumption is that large numbers of minorities will tend to move into areas where (1) minorities already make up 5 to 10 percent of the population; (2) the educational level of the people is relatively low; (3) the income level is relatively low; (4) the percentage of poverty is relatively high; and (5) the value of property is relatively low. The assumption that minority people (regardless of their economic status) will move into areas presently occupied by lower-income Whites is not always accurate.

6. Eleanor P. Wolf, "The Tipping Point in Racially Changing Neighborhoods," in Bernard L. Frieden and Robert Morris, *Urban Planning and Social Policy* (New York: Basic Books, 1976), pp. 148-55.

7. Robert G. Wegman, "Neighborhoods and Schools in Racial Transition," *Growth and Change*, July 1975, p. 5.

8. Gordon E. Nelson, "Some Perspectives on Redlining," in *Redlining: A Special Report by Federal National Mortgage Association*, Washington, D.C., January 1976, p. 11.

Chapter 3. Congregations in Transition

1. Typology from Ezra Earl Jones, *Strategies for New Churches* (New York: Harper & Row, 1976), pp. 37-42.

2. Lyle E. Schaller, *Hey, That's Our Church!* (Nashville: Abingdon Press, 1975), p. 51, 52, 56.

3. Stephen L. Fink, "Crisis and Motivation, a Theoretical Model," *Archives of Physical Medicine and Rehabilitation*, 1967, pp. 952-57.

4. Lawrence Lucas, *Black Priest/White Church: Catholics and Racism* (New York: Random House, 1970), p. 217-18.

5. Speed Leas and Paul Kittlaus, *Church Fights: Managing Conflict in the Local Church* (Philadelphia: Westminster Press, 1973), p. 110-111.

Chapter 4. Transition in the Cities of the 1980s

1. U.S. Census, "Social and Economic Characteristics of the Metropolitan and Non-metropolitan Population: 1977 & 1970."

2. George Sternlieb and Robert W. Lake, "Aging Suburbs and Black Home Ownership," *Annals of the American Academy of Political and Social Science,* November 1975, p. 90.
3. *Ibid.*
4. Peter Z. Snyder, "The Social Environment of the Urban Indian," in Jack O. Waddell and O. Michael Watson, *The American Indian in Urban Society* (Boston: Little, Brown, 1971), p. 218.
5. Quoted in Lou Cannon and Joel Kotkin, "We Belong Here: Hispanics Strive for Assimilation While Retaining Ethnic Identity," *Washington Post,* March 30, 1978.
6. *Guide for Establishing Ethnic Congregations* (Atlanta: Home Mission Board, Southern Baptist Convention, n.d.)
7. J. Thomas Black, Allan Borut, and Robert Dubinsky, *Private-Market Housing Renovation in Older Urban Areas* (Washington, D.C.: The Urban Land Institute, 1977), p. 1.
8. Fred Ferretti, "A Tale of Two Cities: The New and the Old in Hoboken," *New York Times,* January 27, 1979.
9. *Ibid.*
10. *Washington Post,* December 26, 1978.
11. *Ibid.*
12. Wolf Von Eckardt, "Opportunity for a Livable City," *Washington Post,* June 16, 1978.
13. Donna E. Shalala, Assistant Secretary, HUD, quoted in Robert Rhinholdt, "U.S. Housing Study Finds Displacement of Poor in Slums is Minimal," *New York Times,* February 13, 1979.
14. Cited in Jim Wallis, "The New Refugees," *Sojourners,* November 1978, p. 13.
15. John A. Collins, "New Hope for Old Neighborhoods: Redlining vs. Urban Reinvestment," *Christian Century,* March 15, 1978, p. 274.
16. Karen Parker Kuttner, "Four Congregations—One Church," *New World Outlook,* May 1976, p. 24-25.
17. Alston Percel, "Urban Black Church Development," *JSAC Grapevine,* vol. IV, no. 1.
18. Grant S. Shockley, Earl D. C. Brewer, and Marie Townsend, *Black Pastors and Churches in United Methodism* (Atlanta: Center for Research and Social Change, Emory University), pp. 62-63.
19. Robert K. Merton, *Social Theory and Social Structure* (Glencoe, Ill: Free Press, 1957), pp. 424, 432, 436.

Chapter 5. Strategies for Churches

1. B. Carlisle Driggers, *The Church in the Changing Community: Crisis or Opportunity?* (Atlanta: Home Mission Board, Southern Baptist Convention, 1977), p. 37-38.
2. *Ibid.*, p. 38.
3. Charles H. Straut, Jr., "An Advocacy for a Mainline, White Church

Recruitment Policy Among Blacks and Hispanics in Transitional Neighborhoods," D. Min. project, Drew University, March 1977, p. 33-34.

4. Paul Dietterich, "Pre-Transitional Church Development," a report given to the Churches in Transition Project, Community Renewal Society, Chicago, Ill., October 6, 1977.

5. *A Covenant Agreement Relative to the Training Project for Pre-Transitional Churches,* Community Renewal Society, Chicago.

6. *Binding in Covenant Faithful People of All Ages, Tongues, and Races,* Churches in Transition National Consultation Proceedings Document, pp. 47-51.